NOTES &
QUERIES

VOLUME 3

NOTES & QUERIES

VOLUME 3

compiled by

Brian Whitaker

illustrations by

The Senate

FOURTH ESTATE · *London*

First published in Great Britain in 1992 by
Fourth Estate Limited
289 Westbourne Grove
London W11 2QA

Reprinted 1993

*A catalogue record for this book is available from the British
Library*

ISBN 1–85702–052–9

*Typeset by York House Typographic Ltd, London
Printed and bound in Great Britain by
Cox & Wyman Ltd, Reading, Berkshire*

PREFACE

THIS book has not been written by chimpanzees, I can assure you of that. It is, however, entirely possible that it might have been.

Given enough typewriters or word-processors, and enough time, a team of chimpanzees would be quite capable of turning out a book like this, dropping in a few Shakespearian sonnets along the way or even an improved version of Jeffrey Archer's latest blockbuster. (Doubting readers should turn now to page 76 for confirmation.)

The trouble with employing chimpanzees to type at random is that, first of all, they tend to get bits of banana skin stuck between the keys. Secondly, in addition to the literary gems, they also produce an intolerable amount of unreadable rubbish. And finally, they take a somewhat relaxed view of the publisher's deadlines.

Instead, this book has been written by readers of the *Guardian* newspaper – those erudite and often witty people who week after week supply answers to the bizarre questions posed by other readers in the paper's Notes & Queries column.

Such is their enthusiasm that we can now offer a third volume of highlights from that column in more permanent form.

Brian Whitaker

QUESTION: Do clergymen live longer than ordinary mortals?

☐ CLERGY have one of the lowest death rates resulting from industrial accidents and diseases. Per thousand million man hours worked, the numbers of recorded occupational fatalities are: Anglican clergy 10, shopkeepers 30, engineers 100, kings of England 5,000. Drowning in fonts is rare, and martyrdom unfashionable, but falling down steps or into graves, and being struck by falling masonry, are the chief contributors to the statistics for Anglican clergymen. Other denominations may have higher historical rates of martyr-dom but these are sometimes offset by the advantages of working in more modern buildings and graveyards.
Alan M. Calverd, Bishop's Stortford, Herts.

☐ THE first edition of *Inquiries Into Human Faculty* (1883), by Sir Francis Galton, includes a chapter on the 'Objective

Efficacy of Prayer'. This reports the results of a study to
discover whether prayers are answered. Part of the pioneer
statistician's quest was to establish whether the clergy lived
longer than other members of society, given that it is 'their
profession to pray'. An analysis of the mean age attained by
males of various classes who had survived their 30th year
from 1758 to 1843 (deaths by accident and violence
excluded) showed the clergy on 69.49 years, compared with
67.31 for medical men, 68.14 for lawyers and 68.74 for
those in trade and commerce. However, after taking 'the
easy country life and family repose of so many of the clergy'
into account, Galton concluded that 'the prayers of the
clergy for protection against the perils and dangers of the
night, for protection during the day, and for recovery from
sickness, appear to be futile'.
Peter Barnes, Milton Keynes.

☐ IN 1939 Professor J. B. S. Haldane was able to show that
'for a long time Anglican clergymen headed the list [of the
long-lived] but they are now twelfth out of 200, though they
still delay their departure for a better world longer than
clergy of other denominations' (*Science and Everyday Life*).
Haldane also pointed out that the drink trade had the worst
mortality rate (51 per cent above normal) but said nothing
about the life expectancy of bibulous men of the cloth.
J. E. Miller, Brighton, E. Sussex.

**QUESTION: Harry Houdini, the escapologist, wrote
down the secrets of his escapes and had the letters
sealed in a bank vault, not to be opened until 25 years
after his death. Have they now been opened?**

☐ LIKE the story that Houdini drowned during a failed
escape from his notorious Chinese Water Torture Cell, this
delicious rumour is untrue. Houdini was never coy about his
methods; he was an obsessive note-keeper and his writings

on escapology were frequently published during his lifetime. As a magician myself, I would be made to eat worms by my colleagues if I were to give details here, but for anyone genuinely interested, *The Secrets of Houdini* by J. C. Cannell (first published in 1931, just five years after Houdini's death, and reissued in 1973 by Dover Publications) gives a comprehensive account. However, I warn readers that this is a dreary technical book. The real secret of Houdini's success was his mastery of showmanship, and a clever manipulation of the press for maximum publicity.
Tom Cutler, Hove, E. Sussex.

QUESTION: Whoops a daisy! What have daisies got to do with it?

☐ IT IS probably a corrupt form of 'ups-a-daisy', which Chambers defines as an 'interjection of encouragement in lifting a child, or helping to climb'. When I was living in Denmark in the 1950s, I tried to improve my colloquial Danish by reading the comic strips in newspapers. One of these, which I think was called Prince Valiant, was set in the Middle Ages. At one point the hero, on horseback, wants the fair damsel to mount behind him, so he leans down and pulls her up, saying 'Opsedasse!' My inquiries revealed that this was traditionally what an adult said to a small child being lifted on to the adult's knee for a ride ('op' = 'up'; 'dasse' refers to the riding action). The expression later came to be used when an adult was helping a small child to climb a step or when the child had stumbled. Presumably it was brought to England by Danish invaders centuries ago.
Philip Lloyd Lewis, Bournemouth.

QUESTION: What is the process that peas go through to become processed peas?

☐ WHEN I worked in a pea factory as temporary student labour, the process was as follows. The raw material arrived dried from the US. The dried peas were soaked overnight. There was some speculation over how often the soaking medium was changed and what could be found floating in it. Then the soaked peas were blanched in a large metal drum full of steam, and emerged semi-soft and an unappetising yellow colour. They were decanted into their tins and mixed with a vivid green chemical of artificial colouring, artificial mint flavouring (optional), artificial sweetener and preservative. The tins were sealed, pressure-cooked, cooled and labelled. The experience has put me off processed peas for life.

Ian Noble, Middlesbrough, Cleveland.

QUESTION: How long is a biblical cubit?

☐ THE cubit is the distance between the elbow and the tip of the middle finger. Most modern translations of the Bible substitute modern units. For example, the *New English Bible* converts the 'nine cubits' of Deuteronomy 3.11 (the length of the giant King Og's coffin) into 'nearly 14 feet', whereas the *Good News Bible* converts to 'four metres'. What a pity to drop the ancient word! The question remains as to what actual length was used. One calculation is that based on the fact that the Siloam aqueduct was 'in round numbers' 1,200 cubits. Its actual length is 1,750 ft, which is 1,193 cubits of 17.6 in (44.7 cm). However, in the building of the Temple of Solomon in Jerusalem (II Chronicles 3.3) 'cubits of the first measure' are mentioned. This may refer to the Egyptian cubit of 20.63 in (52.4 cm) or to the cubit of Deuteronomy.

Michael L. Cox, Nuneaton, Warwicks.

QUESTION: What is the origin of the expression, 'sent to Coventry'?

☐ THERE are two explanations. In the medieval period Coventry was an important venue for monastic establishments: there were at least six within a five-mile radius of the city. In particular there was a silent order of Carthusian monks, one of only nine in Britain. They were granted land at Charterhouse, just off the London Road. If the London House had a monk among its brethren who found it difficult to adhere to the constraint of silence, the chatterbox was 'sent to Coventry'. There he would have his own small but detached cell, complete with workroom and garden, where silence would be a way of life rather than an imposition. The second, and certainly more popular theory, concerns the Civil War and the Royalist Duke of Hamilton's Scottish soldiers, who were sent as 'prisoners of war' to the parliamentarian city of Coventry. They were held in the disused medieval Bablak Church (now the active Church of St John). As there was little chance of escape outside the city wall, they were allowed to walk around the town during the day. While the citizens did not treat them cruelly, they must have found their Scottish accents and different mode of dress more than a little strange, and preferred to give them a wide berth. This form of cold-shouldering thus led to the modern expression.
Lesley Pritchard, City Guide, Coventry.

QUESTION: Why do gas fires require a flue but gas cookers normally vent their combustion products inside the building?

☐ ALL gas-burning appliances need an adequate supply of fresh air to burn properly, and all produce a small amount of the toxic carbon monoxide gas in the combustion products. If the air supply is restricted, the quantity of carbon monoxide produced rises sharply. The smallest sizes of gas-burning appliances, when burning in a normal room, obtain enough air from gaps around doors, windows, and between floorboards, etc. Appliances rated at 7 kW and above need a fixed air vent and flue to work properly. An exception is made for cookers. This is partly because it would be impractical to fit an effective flue, but also because it is reasonable to assume that people do not leave all the burners on full power for any extended period. It is potentially lethal to use your cooker as a gas fire, with the rings on full for an hour or more and the doors and windows closed. Deaths caused by carbon monoxide poisoning from faulty gas installations occur every winter, but I know of none from a cooker in a house.

A. Tyldesley, Ormskirk, Lancs.

QUESTION: If I stub my toe there is a distinct interval between my being aware of the impact and my feeling the resultant pain. Why aren't the two sensations felt simultaneously?

☐ DIFFERENT sensations travel by different pathways in the nervous system. 'Sensation' is made up of the following so-called modalities: temperature, pain, light, touch, vibration and muscle/joint position-sense. Two different types of nerve pathway carry these modalities, with only a little overlap. All muscle/joint position-sense and vibration enter the 'dorsal columns', so called because the fibres are at the back of the spinal cord. These pathways are well insulated and have very few nerve junctions to contend with, and therefore impulses travel quickly to the brain. The other nerve pathways, the spinothalamic tracts, carry the rest of light–touch sensation, as well as all pain and temperature sensation. The spinothalamic tracts are not so well insulated, have more nerve junctions, take a rather more meandering path to the brain than the dorsal columns and are

relatively old in evolutionary terms. The first sensation likely to be perceived on stubbing the toe is that of some touch, with or without altered joint position-sense. This travels along the dorsal columns and thus arrives at the brain quickly. Later, the rest of touch and all the pain arrives by the spinothalamic tracts. Some pain goes more directly to the brain than the rest of it, which takes a longer detour through the hypothalamus where the emotions get a chance to be involved. This accounts for why you get upset if you stub your toe. But what I find really impressive is how the brain can deal with all this and yet simultaneously work out an appropriately profane expletive ready to be yelled out just as the real pain arrives.
(Dr) Chris Ainsworth, Ramsbottom, Lancs.

☐ THE governing principle is the distance from the body part stubbed to the brain. It may be recalled that bronto-sauruses had to have an auxiliary brain in the pelvic area, otherwise the transmission of information about pain in the brontosaurus tail having become entangled in the plates of a stegosaurus, say, might have taken as long as three days to reach the creature's main brain. If the frequency of toe-stubbing on uneven paving stones is a reliable indicator, it seems probable that mankind, in the interests of self-preser-vation, will evolve an auxiliary pain centre in the pelvic region.
John Davis, Oxford.

QUESTION: If I stick a reply-paid envelope on to a brick, is the recipient liable for the postage?

☐ THIS seems a drastic solution to the problem of junk mail. We have taken to tipping the contents of our dustpan into the prepaid envelope with a note saying: 'Thanks for send-ing us your junk. Here is some of ours.'
Jerry Conway, Kidderminster, Worcs.

QUESTION: Has anybody actually seen a person with a sandwich board proclaiming: 'The end of the world is nigh'?

☐ AS a schoolboy more than 70 years ago I used to go to Fratton Park to watch Portsmouth Football Club, and on match days there was always a sandwich-board man at the Frogmore Road entrance proclaiming: 'The end of the world is nigh.' There was also one outside the Central Hall, Westminster, during the 1944 Labour Party Conference.
Ian Mikardo, London NW8.

QUESTION: What is the truth about solar flares affecting computers? We were recently warned about a gigantic flare, and since then my PCs have given me strange messages.

☐ SOLAR flares produce X-rays (which travel at the speed of light) and sometimes they are associated with enhanced ejection of charged particles (which travel more slowly, at a few hundred kilometres per second). The X-rays produce ionisation when they reach the Earth's upper atmosphere, eight minutes after leaving the Sun. The particles can trigger a complex sequence of events; that is, provided they hit the Earth following their journey from the Sun, which lasts for a few days. These effects include the intensification and Equator-ward motion of the aurora, associated with which are 'electrojet' currents in the upper atmosphere. These can cause rapid fluctuations of a few micro-tesla in the magnetic field at the Earth's surface, but this is only a few per cent of the ambient field. It is very difficult to see how these small fluctuations could affect a personal computer, especially when cased in a metal box. However, it is known that the electrojets do induce very big effects, particularly in operational systems of great length such as power lines and oil pipelines. Indeed, the big disturbance of 13–14 March

1989 influenced many PCs by causing power failures throughout a large area of Canada. The same disturbance brought the aurora to the south of England. In space, the energetic charged particles responsible for the aurora are very hazardous for even 'radiation-hardened' electronics. It is in this hostile environment that satellites have to operate. We should be grateful that the atmosphere shields us and our PCs from these particles, and in doing so generates the astonishing beauty of the aurora.

Mike Lockwood, World Data Centre for Solar Terrestrial Physics, Rutherford Appleton Laboratory, Didcot, Oxon.

☐ ONE effect is the production of ions of elements such as carbon, oxygen and iron, which have energies equivalent to acceleration in voltages up to seven hundred million volts. When particles like these, moving at perhaps half the speed of light, pass through matter they slow down, liberating electrical charge as they go. They readily penetrate the structures of satellites and if they pass through the 'bits' on an electronic chip they can cause a corruption of the computer program or in the contents of a memory. Luckily for our Earth-bound computers, the Earth's atmosphere absorbs virtually all these nasty particles, while the Earth's magnetic field also helps by deflecting them away. Nuclear interactions between these particles and the atmosphere produce showers of other exotic particles. Even in the absence of solar events, there is a continuous low-level flux of very energetic 'Galactic Cosmic Ray' particles in space around us and penetrating into the upper atmosphere. These cause just the same kinds of problems. As with the magnetic effects mentioned by Mike Lockwood, it is difficult to see how the negligibly low numbers of particles reaching the Earth's surface could cause any problems to PCs, particularly at UK latitudes. It is, of course, of increasing concern for highflying aircraft and satellites. Numerous occurrences of 'single-event upsets', as these induced errors are called, were reported on satellites during the large March and June flares earlier this year.

Eamonn Daly, European Space Agency, Noordwijk, Netherlands.

QUESTION: British Rail goods wagons often have the names of fish written on their side. What is the function of this labelling system, and why fish?

☐ IT IS simply a handy way of identifying varieties of wagon. It's much easier to say 'whale', for example, than '50-ton Bogie ballast hopper wagon'. The naming system originates from the period between 1880 and 1950 when urgent messages had to be sent by telegraph. These were coded in order to minimise the number of words transmitted. In Scott's *Shipowners' Telegraphic Manual* of 1899, for example, 'juggernaut' was a shorthand way of saying: 'The crew

# #

# #

scheme evolved by the railways, fish names were simply one
category. Animal and bird names were used for messages
concerning freight; vegetable and fruit names referred to
passenger traffic; and rivers, among others things, were for
general messages. Reptile and insect names, as well as fish,
identified types of rolling stock. Nowadays names are only
seen on wagons controlled by the civil engineers' department (mainly for track and bridge maintenance) and
include the additions 'tope' and 'zander'. These are used
alongside the recent three-letter codes (e. g. YHA) which
allow BR's TOPS computer system to identify wagon types.
Graham Bird, London W4.

**QUESTION: In 1914, who said of the First World War,
'It'll be over by Christmas'?**

☐ FIELD-Marshal Sir John Denton French, the commander-
in-chief of the British Expeditionary Force in France. His
view was fiercely opposed by Lord Kitchener, and French
later resigned after being criticised as indecisive.
Mike Hurley, Doncaster, S. Yorks.

**QUESTION: How are members of an orchestra paid?
Does a percussionist who gives a couple of 'pings' on a
triangle get the same amount as a violinist who beavers
away for hours?**

☐ THE reason why all orchestra members are entitled to the
same amount is that it is the composer who has decided how
much or how little the individual instruments are to do.
Every member of the orchestra will be required at all
rehearsals, the entire performance and promotional exercises. This means that the commitment of all orchestra
members is identical. However, the comparison between a

percussionist and a violinist is particularly unfair. Percussionists have long been on the receiving end of such humour (What do you call someone who always hangs around musicians? A percussionist). The job requirements go far beyond the playing of a few 'pings'. Even if the part is that simple, the percussionist has to count many bars of rest to ensure that the said 'pings' come at the correct moment. The counting requires more concentration than actually playing. Remember also that percussionists are the only orchestral musicians required to change instruments and even play more than one instrument at a time. Also, at the end of the concert, the violinists and trumpeters simply pop their instruments into their cases and head for the bar. The percussionist has to lug out drums, timpani and all manner of assorted burdens; often single-handed, always thirsty. *Gordon Livesey, Chaffers Mead, Surrey.*

☐ IN Britain there are two categories of orchestra: those employing players on a full-time contract and those hiring players on a session basis. The first category includes all the regional symphony orchestras (CBSO, Halle, etc.), opera and ballet orchestras (ENO, Royal Opera, etc.) and the BBC orchestras. These usually pay players a salary, plus holiday and sick pay, and operate a contributory pension scheme. Those in the second category pay their musicians fees for each session worked. In all orchestras players are ranked either as section leader, principal, sub-principal or tutti (also known as rank and file). Minimum salaries and fees are agreed between the Musicians' Union and orchestra managers. Salaries and fees of tutti players are usually the lowest of the four groups, so by definition a percussion player will receive more than an equally experienced string player, the theory being that the higher rate of pay should reflect the responsibility of performing parts of a more exposed nature. *Christopher Clift, Violinist, Birmingham 11.*

QUESTION: Where can I learn Volapuk, the artificial language and forerunner of Esperanto?

□ THE only way you can learn it now is from a book. This language project was the work of Johann Martin Schleyer (1831–1912), whose 1880 textbook, *Volapuk die Weltsprache*, was reissued, edited by R. Haupenthal, in 1982 (George Olms Verlag, Hildesheim/Zurich/New York). It is in German; there is no English textbook. Virtually the only people interested in Volapuk these days are Esperantologists. The first Esperanto local group (Nuremberg, 1888) was a former Volapuk society and by the turn of the century Esperanto had effectively killed Volapuk. One reason may have been the proprietorial attitude of Schleyer to his work, as contrasted with Zamenhof's insistence that Esperanto did not belong to him, as author, but to all mankind. The consequence today is that there are hundreds of thousands of speakers of Esperanto around the world and a flourishing movement of supporters. But there are no Volapukists left. *J. C. Wells, Professor of Phonetics, University College, London.*

□ THE inventor, Monsignor Schleyer, had no grasp of the practicalities of creating a language. Instead of jettisoning unnecessary complications which many modern languages happily dispense with, he built up a hopelessly complex structure of moods, tenses and cases until his language was actually more complex than classical Latin. He also applied bizarre rules in his choice of words. For example, no word could contain the letter 'R' because some nations had difficulty distinguishing it from 'L'. Thus Volapuk was made up from the word 'vol' (that's 'world' without the 'W' and 'R', which are difficult for some people, and without the 'D', for no particular reason); then the letter 'A' to mark the genitive; and finally 'speak' (without the initial 'S', which worries some nations, and with 'U' instead of 'EA'). Hardly surprisingly, the first Congress of Volapukists was also the

last. The participants found that they could not speak the language and that when they attempted to do so nobody understood them.
Dermond Quirke, Halifax, Yorks.

☐ A STARTING point is the 60-page *Grammar of Volapuk* by W. A. Seret, published in 1887 and reprinted in 1988. I obtained my copy earlier this year from Joseph Biddulph, Languages Information Centre, 32 Stryd Ebeneser, Pontypridd, CF37 5PB.
Paul Gibbins, Congleton, Cheshire.

☐ VOLAPUK ai lifon, do smaliko, ed ob binob nu Cifal mufa. (Volapuk lives, though on-a-small-scale, and I am now the-president of-the-movement.) If anyone wishes to learn the language through books or tapes, let him or her contact me.
Brian R. Bishop, Cifal Volapukamufa, 155 Leighton Ave, Leigh-on-Sea, Essex SS9 1PX.

QUESTION: Judas received 30 pieces of silver for betraying Jesus. What would the equivalent sum be today?

☐ IF THE silver pieces were denarii, each of them a day's wage for a Roman soldier, 30 would be the equivalent of a month's wages, in modern terms about £1,000–£1,500. A similar conversion rate helps with the story of the widow's mite: her offering, comprising 'two coins, together worth a farthing' (*New English Bible*) was worth one 32nd of a denarius, about a fiver nowadays, and exactly the sort of sum which would appear insignificant to the rich but could be all a pensioner has to live on for several days.
Edward Hughes, London E8.

☐ ACCORDING to Matthew's gospel, Judas returned the money to the chief priests in a fit of remorse. Rather than

replace such a tainted sum in the treasury of the temple, the elders used it to buy 'the potter's field, to bury strangers in'. It seems, therefore, that the money was sufficient to purchase a plot of land suitable for use as a cemetery. All we need do now is look at a modern valuation for a cemetery, taken from a recent transaction, say that conducted by Westminster Council, and we can describe the value of 30 pieces of silver as 15 pence.
A. J. Robinson, London E17.

QUESTION: One of Jack Kerouac's novels is entitled *Desolation Angels*. From where does the term originate?

☐ ON ONE level 'Desolation' refers to Desolation Peak in Oregon, where Kerouac went trekking and spent 63 days as a forest fire look-out. In the same way as in *On the Road*, the journey and stay were symbolic of spiritual development and a religious retreat. 'Angels' refers to Kerouac and the relatively small circle of American beatniks. 'Beat' means both moving with the pulse of jazz and life and also 'beato', or blessed and angelic (cf. the 'angel-headed hipsters' of Allen Ginsberg's 'Howl'). 'Desolation' also refers to the spiritually moribund state of American society, with the angel beatniks pointing the way back home to God. The beatniks of the 1940s were the first to sense the glimmerings of the current New Age mysticism.
Paul Woodcraft, Ardullie, Ross-shire.

QUESTION: Why is no food blue?

☐ THIS is not quite true: a limited number of edibles can be found in this hue. In the search for true blue foods it is important to discount impostors like blueberries, blue cheese and Blue Nun wine, which never live up to their names and are usually grey or purple. There is, however, a variety of American corn known as blue corn, which can be obtained in some shops in the form of tortilla chips which are not only convincingly blue but surprisingly delicious. For the most impressive edible deep blue colour you have to venture into the world of fresh wild fungi. When the flesh of many varieties of Boletus is broken or cut and exposed to the air the off-yellow flesh immediately turns a dark royal blue. Unfortunately this spectacular pigment is destroyed by cooking, so they would have to be served raw if you wanted to give the impression of having spilt ink over the salad. For some wonderful photographs of blue fungi see *Mushrooms*, by Roger Phillips.

Alasdair Friend, Edinburgh.

☐ ALASDAIR Friend cites 'blue corn' (maize) as an example of blue food. This is not so simple. The maize grain is pinkish in colour until it is treated with a preparation of wood ashes, which turns it blue. This is but one example of a large range of plant pigments of the anthocyanin family, which are pink when acid and blue when alkaline. Since most plant foods are mildly acidic when fresh, anthocyanin-coloured foods are very rarely seen in their blue form. To see this effect very simply, try adding sodium bicarbonate (alkali) to chopped red cabbage, and then reversing the effect with vinegar or lemon juice (acid).

Erica Wheeler, London School of Hygiene and Tropical Medicine, University of London.

☐ THE answer given by Alasdair Friend neglects the fact that blue food is not normally attractive to humans. Fifteen years ago I spent a year at the Australian scientific base at Mawson, Antarctica. As the base was cut off for most of the year, the cook had to bake bread for about 30 people. He occasionally got fed up with baking every morning and he would add a few drops of blue dye to the dough. Although in all other respects the bread was exactly the same, hardly

anyone could bring himself to eat it and the cook had a
couple of mornings free from baking while the blue bread
went stale. If anyone complained, he just said that the blue
bread was perfectly edible, as indeed it was.
P. M. Davies, Newport, Gwent.

**QUESTION: On a crossing controlled by traffic lights,
can a pedestrian get the lights to change more quickly
by repeated pressing of the button?**

☐ No. The first push of the button will register the presence
of a pedestrian (acknowledged by the illumination of a
'wait' sign) and initiate the process to change the lights. The
time the pedestrian has to wait varies. It often depends on
the time elapsed since the last 'green man' signal, because
the lights are designed to provide the optimal distribution of
time between pedestrians and vehicles. If the lights have not
changed for a while, the response to pushing the button may
be instant; otherwise, the pedestrian may have to wait up to
40 seconds. Other factors which may influence the wait
time, depending on the complexity of the installation, are
the weight of traffic and whether or not the crossing is linked
to other signals nearby. Pushing the button when the 'wait'
sign is already illuminated will have no effect. It may,
however, make pedestrians feel they are in control of events
or simply help release frustration – it does for me, anyway.
John Vincent, Transportation Planning Associates, York.

**QUESTION: Olives (and olive oil) are often described as
'good for you'. What are their magic properties?**

☐ STUDIES among southern European countries, where a
Mediterranean-style diet is consumed, have shown low incidence of coronary heart disease. Such diets are typically
high in mono-unsaturated fats, particularly oleic acid (which

comes mainly from olive oil), and moderately low in poly-unsaturated fats (PUFAs). Recent research has also shown that mono-unsaturates are as effective as PUFAs in lowering plasma cholesterol. Work done in the US (by Mattson and Grundy), in Holland (by Mensink and Katan) and in Canada (by McDonald and Associates) has shown that oleic acid is effective in lowering plasma total cholesterol and low-density lipoprotein (LDL) cholesterol. Mono-unsaturated fatty acids have also been shown to be more effective at maintaining high-density lipoprotein (HDL) levels, while PUFAs have been shown, when taken in large quantities, to lower HDL. High levels of blood cholesterol, particularly LDL cholesterol, constitute a major risk factor for coronary heart disease. Experts agree that dietary levels of saturated fats, which are high in cholesterol, should be reduced. Olive oil contains more oleic acid and a higher percentage of mono-unsaturated fatty acids than any other dietary fat.

Niki Georgiou, the Olive Oil Bureau, London WC1.

□ THE main reason we are told foods are good for us is when they taste unpleasant. Nobody ever says: 'If you're good I'll give you some sprouts, now eat that ice-cream because it's good for you.' Olives are the fruit of *Oliva europaea* and – in the fresh state – are bitter and inedible. Before sale they are steeped in water and salt solutions to remove excess bitterness. The oil is obtained by pressure and is one of the lightest cooking oils. It is also remarkably resistant to the effects of heat.

Brian J. Ford, London SW1.

QUESTION: Inside London Underground trains there are various letters, e.g. EPBIV, BRV, EL. What do they mean?

□ THESE abbreviations are known as the Cant Rail Code.

They indicate where certain pieces of equipment for use in the case of defects or emergencies may be found. EPBIV means Electro-Pneumatic Brake Isolating Valve, BRV Brake Release Valve and EL Emergency Ladder.

Tony Roberts, Train Driver, Piccadilly Line Depot, London W3.

QUESTION: What is the origin of the mortar-board headgear worn by graduates?

☐ IN THE European universities of the twelfth century it was customary to award the graduating scholar a special cap, which was known variously as a *pileus* or biretta. It appears originally to have been a plain round bonnet crowned with a small tuft, or apex, and was worn over a skull-cap or coif. Around the year 1500 it became fashionable to pinch the crown of the cap into four corners, allegedly to represent the sign of the cross (universities were ultimately under the authority of the Pope). This came to be known as the *pileus quadratus* ('square cap'), and was referred to in English as the cater-cap or corner-cap. In some instances the cap developed into a more rigid, formalised headgear. Among Catholic clerics it became the biretta, still worn today, and the fins on its crown recall the quartering on the original *pileus*. Meanwhile in England, by the end of the seventeenth century, in the academic world the same cap had been reduced to a square of pasteboard covered with black serge and attached to a rigid skull-cap. This was the forerunner of the modern mortar-board. The original soft, flat cap is still worn by many female graduates and by female members of numerous church choirs.

J. P. Fortune, London SW6.

QUESTION: Are the star dates in the Captain's Log in *Star Trek* in any chronological order?

☐ IN THE original TV series the star dates were meant to be chronological, but delays in production of specific episodes, scheduling considerations, poor editing of scripts, etc., soon meant that star dates effectively became random numbers. There have been attempts to rationalise these dates along 'scientific' lines, where the date is explained to take account of faster-than-light travel and relativity. Some fans have adopted the international year–month–day–time format to try to explain the TV dates. However, none of these works for all the star dates in series. In the new TV series the star dates have the following format: $4Xyyy.yy$ where the 4 denotes the twenty-fourth century, X the season (1 for the first, 2 for the second – currently showing – 3 for the third, etc.) and $yyy.yy$ is a number between 000.00 and 999.99 to indicate the 'day'. However, this means that there are 1,000 'days' in a 'year' and only 10 'years' in a 'century'. Thus although a 'year' is more than three times longer than a solar year, a 'century' is less than a third the length of a solar century.

Chris Forman, Nottingham.

QUESTION: Who was St Ivel?

☐ 'IVEL' comes from the Saxon name for Yeovil, Givele, which appears in the Domesday Book. The saintly prefix was added in 1901 by William Henry Barrett of Aplin & Barrett, who linked the name to an imaginary local order of monks possessed of fabled recipes. The first product to bear the new trademark was lactic cheese, which some of your older readers may remember for its distinctive dark blue box.

Kathy Cuddihy, St Ivel Ltd, Swindon, Wilts.

☐ HE (or she) is a bogus saint, dreamed up by the devisers of the trademark. At the time of the mark's registration, there was a vogue for religious product names, viz. that other

bogus saint, Bruno, and his genuine colleague, St Julien
(though I doubt if the latter smoked).
Stephen Allcroft, North Tyneside, Tyne and Wear.

☐ IN DISCUSSING the bogus St Ivel, Stephen Allcroft does an
injustice to St Bruno, about whom there is nothing bogus
except perhaps the connection with pipe tobacco. Bruno
(1033–1101) was the founder of the reclusive Carthusian
order and, although never formally canonised – since the
Carthusians discourage public honours – he was allowed a
feast day (6 October) in 1514. Bruno once wrote: 'Only
those who have experienced it can know the benefit and
delight to be had from the quietness and solitude of an
hermitage.' It is this connection with mellow contemplation
which presumably attracted the tobacco company to adopt
his name. The words would certainly sound well in the
rounded tones of an Anthony Hopkins voice-over.
Justin Potts, London WC1.

**QUESTION: How popular was the Christian name
Adolf in German-speaking countries before 1945?
What about since?**

☐ THERE are no national statistics but statistics relating to
individual boroughs. For example, in Mannheim, 1.6 per
cent of boys were named Adolf before 1880 (as compared to
the most popular name, Karl, with 10.3 per cent). In 1880
and shortly after, Adolf rose to 2.2 per cent, falling again to
1.0 per cent in 1923. Statistics for nine boroughs in eastern
Germany show Adolf occurring seven times in 1924 (with
the most popular name, Heinz, appearing 247 times). In
1934 – one year after Hitler's rise to power – it occurred 37
times (while Gunther was most popular, at 145 times). In
1944 no one was named Adolf, and the same is true for
1954, 1964 and 1969. One researcher, Rosa Katz, inquired
in 1938 at the registry office of Baden-Baden. She found six

boys named Adolf and one Adolf-Benito out of a total of 641. She did the same at Rostock in 1938 and found five out of a total of 2,728. Thus, in line with other Germanic names, Adolf was losing ground before Hitler's rise to power. During the Hitler era it experienced a modest, short-lived boom and then disappeared.

(Dr) Arne Holtorf, Deutsches Seminar der Universität Tübingen, Germany.

☐ WHEN you name a baby in Germany you are required by law to choose a name appropriate to the child's sex. About 200 suitable names are helpfully suggested on the reverse side of the birth registration form. Adolf is not included in this otherwise quite comprehensive list. The name is not only less popular than it used to be, it has even ceased to exist officially. Incidentally, in the current Munich telephone directory there is no one between Hitl, J. and Hitsch, C.

J. A., Munich, Germany.

QUESTION: In the Constable exhibition at the Tate Gallery there are no paintings or drawings depicting winter scenes. Did he paint winter subjects, and if not, is it because of the discomfort of sitting outside in winter or because he had a romanticised view of the countryside as eternally green?

☐ CONSTABLE not only concentrated on just one time of year (summer) but also on one time of day (noon). His reply to his friends' complaints about this lack of variety was, essentially, that to achieve greatness in the treatment of any subject, the artist has to keep plugging away at it. Perhaps this was based on his belief that landscape painting is (as he put it) 'scientific as well as poetic'. He tried to achieve a complete understanding of his subject matter ('We see nothing until we truly understand it'); like a scientist, he chose a narrow area that he could research in depth. But he

supported research into other areas: he admired a snow
scene by Ruisdael enough to make a full-size copy of it and
he loved the evocation of the harshness of winter which
opens James Thomson's poem, *The Seasons*. He certainly
did not present an 'idealised' countryside, if that means one
with all the nasty bits left out. Details in his pictures clearly
imply that all that fruitfulness is the result of heavy rain and
hard work – one reason, perhaps, why he rarely sold a
picture. And many of his later paintings have a harder,
bleaker mood. One can still ask: 'Why summer?' Among
several probable reasons, I would emphasise the simple fact
that human activity, or signs of it, was more visible in
summer. For religious reasons, he wanted to show the
country as a place of interaction between human and
natural processes, and this would be less clear in other
seasons.
Hudson Pace, London SW11.

□ BY CHOOSING the middle of the day in the middle of the
year, in the middle of the working week in East Anglia, he
was not encouraging a romanticised or idealised view of
anything, and he would expect his viewers to know that
leaves fell off trees.
R. A. Johnson, Wickwar, Glos.

□ WINTER subjects are missing from the Tate show but it is
untrue that Constable restricted himself to summer and
noon subjects. Leslie, his biographer, suggests of *The Ceno-
taph* (not on show) that 'Constable had consulted [Sir
George Beaumont] in choosing the autumnal tints for the
foliage of [this] scene . . . but his doing so arose naturally
from his having made his studies of it late in the autumn'.
Also, look through the show or catalogue for 'the same' tree
appearing in states of foliage suggestive of different seasons.
The claim that Constable depicted only noontime is bizarre.
I opened the catalogue at random and hit upon *Hampstead
Heath – Sun Setting over Harrow*. Practical reasons for

neglect of winter scenes are not hard to find. It is not irrelevant that Cézanne, that hardy observer of the motif, painted his *Melting Snow at Fontainebleau* from a photograph (Rewald's biography).
Paul S. Griffiths, Fulham, London.

QUESTION: Do wasps serve any useful purpose?

☐ WASPS are predators of flies and caterpillars. One wasp may make several predatory expeditions an hour. One nest could contain a couple of thousand adult hunters. That's a lot fewer caterpillars and flies in a garden, even after one day. Wasps can convert your garden fence into a three-dimensional paper architecture that can support at least 10 times its own weight. That seems to me worth a round of applause. One wasp can provoke limb-flailing frenzy in a creature 100,000 times its own size, a defensive, yes defensive, advantage that should impress any military strategist. Wasp grubs are the favoured diet of that strange bird of prey, the honey buzzard *(Pernis apivorus)* – long may it survive. Even if you are decidedly against wasps, at least learn to respect the enemy. There are possibly a thousand species of social wasps worldwide. Their colonies range in size from two adults to about one million (yes, a million wasps estimated in one nest of a South American species). In Britain we have seven species of wasps: the hornet, *Vespa crabro* (only in southern England and becoming rarer), two species of Dolichovespula (square-faced, rather ignorant-looking, making nests with narrow horizontal bands) and four species of Vespula with prettier, heart-shaped faces and nests that are a mosaic of shell-like patterns. So, next time you get stung cry 'Hallelujah, the world would be a duller place without wasps!'
(Dr) M. H. Hansell, Dept of Zoology, University of Glasgow.

☐ WASPS are agents from outer space appointed to keep an

eye on the progress of human beings. They soon discovered that human beings didn't serve any useful purpose on the planet so they turned their attention to rotting plums and open-air cream teas and have been having a whale of a time ever since.

M. R. Meek, Norwich, Norfolk.

□ THE Kayapo Indians of the Brazilian Amazon use wasps to protect their crops from leaf-cutting ants. The wasps prefer certain types of banana tree for nesting. The Indians plant these trees around the edges of their fields and among the crops, thus ensuring a domestic force of wasps to deal with the ants. This is a most effective and ecologically harmless system of dealing with a serious pest.

Alfred Willetts, Broughton, Chester.

□ THE parasitic wasp, *Encarsia formosa*, is commercially available for the control of whitefly in greenhouses. The only other control method is to spray with pesticides every couple of days, with all that implies in terms of residues in crops. These wasps are available from any good organic gardening supplier, notably the Henry Doubleday Research Association at Ryton-on-Dunsmore, Coventry, CV8 3LG.

Tony Green, Rochdale, Lancs.

QUESTION: In French it's 'impasse'; in English it's 'cul-de-sac', which, if it means anything, means 'bag's bottom'. Can anyone explain?

□ CUL-DE-SAC, meaning 'dead-end road', was in use in France in the eighteenth century and you will find the expression in several novels of the period. My *Petit Robert* also quotes Victor Hugo using it in this context. Presumably, we picked it up in this country sometime after that, while the French moved on to the more modern impasse (which, of course, we use too, meaning 'deadlock'). Cul-de-sac, or

'bottom of the bag', is a wonderfully graphic expression for a dead end, something you go down and can't find the way out of.
Claire Watts, London.

☐ I CANNOT explain cul-de-sac but I can quote a similar example of what I call a 'false Gallicism' which may shed some light on the matter. Brassière, authentic French for 'child's sleeved vest', is a false Gallicism for authentic French *soutien-gorge*, meaning literally, 'throat support' (French female anatomy seems to differ from its English counterpart). As far as I know, there is no English word for brassière. Perhaps we could follow the German *Büstenhalter* ('bust-holder').
Joseph Witriol, Fellow of the Institute of Linguists Translator, London N12.

QUESTION: What is the origin of the name 'Spike' as in Spike Milligan and Spike Lee?

☐ IN JAZZ circles double bass players were sometimes nick-named Spike – for obvious reasons. An early example (*circa* 1930) was Spike Hughes, the British musician who recorded some of his charming jazz pieces with Benny Carter's orchestra, led another recording band known as the Deccadents, wrote a column in the *Melody Maker* under the pseudonym 'Mike' and achieved respectability as an opera critic. Spike Heatley of the Be-Bop Preservation Society is also a bass player but I believe that Spike Jones, who led the City Slickers, was a drummer.
(Prof.) Syd Urry, Bridport, Dorset.

QUESTION: In a recent accident I cut a fingertip deeply and bound the flap of flesh with adhesive plaster so that

it would re-knit. I have since been told that 'super-glue' serves well in this situation. Is it advisable?

□ THERE is a medical 'super-glue' which is used for skin closure in certain situations. It is not the same as ordinary 'super-glue' and is sterile. Using ordinary 'super-glue' at home to mend a skin wound is not advisable for several reasons. Firstly, the glue may be dirty, and there is a risk that a thick layer put over a cut would lead to an underlying infection. Secondly, the glue itself can damage skin cells, and on application it produces some heat of reaction which will also destroy cells. If the skin cells at the edge of the wound die, then the cut will take much longer to heal. Thirdly, although 'super-glue' is supposed to produce a permanent bond, if regularly exposed to soap and water, the seal will disintegrate. The ideal method of closing a fingertip laceration is to use adhesive strips sold especially for this purpose. A small gap should be left between each strip to allow any exudate to escape and the wound should be kept clean and dry.
R. J. Morton, MRCP FRCS, Consultant in Accident and Emergency, Manchester Royal Infirmary.

□ THERE has been extensive research of the use of this glue in surgical operations, especially for joining cut ends of bowel, which are notoriously prone to leaking. As a GP my experience is limited to superficial wounds. A neighbouring practice routinely uses it for head wounds with 'clean' edges. My one attempt resulted in an unusually close and lasting contact with the patient which was welcome to neither of us.
(Dr) Frances Szekely, Chatteris, Cambs.

□ WHILE unable to offer medical advice, I can comment on its use on finger injuries sustained while rock climbing. The small, often sharp, holds used on modern climbs regularly rip flaps of skin from climbers' fingertips – described as 'ripping a flapper' by the climbing fraternity. Using 'super-

glue' to re-attach the offending 'flapper' enables a climber to continue, rather than skulk off to wait for the wound to heal. While effective, the technique does involve some pain and is normally accompanied by running in small circles with the damaged digit held aloft. As to whether the 'super-glue' aids climbing performance I have no reliable information.
Geoff Smallwood, Staines, Middx.

QUESTION: How did the Odeon cinema chain get its name?

☐ AS THE eldest son of the founder, Oscar Deutsch, I am able to tell you with authority that the name was derived from my late father's initials and colleagues' references to 'OD on the Board', etc. To back this up, the first letters were also taken from 'Oscar Deutsch Entertains Our Nation'. The first Odeon cinema was built at Perry Barr in 1930 and when my father died at the age of 48 in December 1941 he had built up a chain of cinemas comprising both Paramount and Gaumont totalling 320.
R. L. Deutsch, Deutsch Metals, Ilmington, Warwicks.

☐ THE name comes from the Greek *odeion*, which means 'song place' (which in turn comes from the Greek *ode*, meaning 'song'), and was applied in ancient times to theatres where musical performances were held. The most famous of these is the Odeon of Herodeus Atticus, on the slopes below the Acropolis in Athens, which is still used for son-et-lumière and other performances. The application to cinemas in the 1930s was presumably part of the general attempt to give an upmarket feel to mass entertainment, and the use of classical architectural styles for interior designs within the art deco buildings was commonly found. Other examples of this are the use of 'Lyceum' for ballrooms (taken from the name of the garden in Athens where Aristotle taught), and the incorporation of ancient Egyptian

motifs into the otherwise art deco designs of some of the
Burton tailoring stores.
Chris Ferrary, Chartered Town Planner, London E17.

**QUESTION: My son insists that there is a school in this
country where boys wear short trousers up to the age of
18. Can anyone confirm this?**

☐ IT IS Keil School, an independent, secondary, coeduca-
tional, boarding/day school in the west of Scotland. Shorts,
which were once a compulsory part of the uniform, are now
optional but many boys (age range 10–18) opt to wear
shorts in preference to longs – even on the frostiest of winter
mornings. Quite simply, they find them comfortable – as do
a great many boys and men living in warmer climates. On
more formal occasions, the boys at Keil wear kilts.
C. H. Tongue, Headmaster, Keil School, Dumbarton.

☐ AT SEDBERGH School, Cumbria, short trousers were *de
rigueur* until 1974. Long trousers were introduced then
because pupils apparently felt they were the objects of
ridicule. As a former pupil of Giggleswick School (a more
forward-thinking establishment nearby, where such bizarre
fetishes were eschewed), I have to confirm that their fears
were well founded.
David Stockdale, Macclesfield, Cheshire.

**QUESTION: Would it be better for the environment if I
were buried or cremated when I die?**

☐ UNDOUBTEDLY, yes.
Ray Jenkin, Cardiff.

☐ NO ONE, as far as I am aware, has quantified or queried the
fuel used for cremation. Nor has anyone questioned the

possible pollutants emitted during cremation in this country. A recent study of these gases in Switzerland (see the journal *Nature*, 1991, vol. 349, pp. 746–7) shows that lead and mercury are given off during the crematory process. The mercury probably comes from alloys used in tooth fillings, but no explanation has been found for the lead. Therefore the most environmentally friendly method of disposal is to be buried in a perishable coffin which decays in the soil and allows the body to be broken down into its constituent minerals. This would include the mercury from fillings. After a period of 10 years or so the grave space may be re-used, thereby demolishing the argument that cemeteries inevitably use up increasing areas of land. I claim no originality for this idea. Sir Francis Seymour Haden (1818–1910) devised it in the late nineteenth century as a riposte to the arguments used by the Cremation Society. When Haden died he was buried in a disposable, or 'earth to earth', coffin at Brookwood.
John Clarke, Sheffield.

☐ THERE are recycling implications, too. I would refer enquirers to the full-length version of the song 'Ilkley Moor' for an examination of those questions.
Brian J. Ford, London SW1.

QUESTION: Why are burglars always depicted by cartoonists as wearing striped polo-neck jerseys?

☐ THIS originated at the end of the eighteenth century. Royal Navy sailors, whose uniform after about 1790 comprised the distinctive striped jersey, were notoriously ill-treated and often forced into crime upon their discharge from service. The issue was particularly topical during the period coinciding with the heyday of political satire. The inevitable black mask, covering the eyes alone, is the satirical key, emphasising the inadequacy of the disguise. The

bag marked 'swag' appears to have been a Victorian addition.
Richard James, Woodbridge, Suffolk.

QUESTION: At 6 p.m. on 18 July my watch was one second slow by the chimes of Big Ben on BBC radio. Checks with the time signals showed my watch to be accurate. Is Big Ben broadcast live or does the BBC occasionally mistime a recording?

☐ BIG BEN is live when broadcast on radio; it is used on Radio 4 to introduce both the six o'clock news and the midnight news. It can be an extremely awkward beast because, being a mechanical clock mechanism and an old one at that, it is prone to small variations. The chimes preceding the hourly strikes can begin anywhere between 25 and 18 seconds before the hour, although the strikes themselves are rarely more than a second out. This can provide peculiar problems for Radio 4 newsreaders, who are expected to announce the news bulletin in the small gap between the chimes and the first strike with the words 'BBC news at midnight, this is Malcolm Gaud' (or whoever). There can be heart-stopping moments, and pregnant pauses, waiting for Big Ben to speak, with the newsreader treading delicately through a minefield of unpredictable chimes and strikes.
Malcolm Gaud, BBC, London W1.

☐ EVEN if recorded, there would be no guarantee that Big Ben would be played at the right time. Radio 4's pips are one second slower than BBC Ceefax's clock, which is one second slower than the clock on Oracle teletext, which in turn is no less than 1.5 seconds faster than BT's Speaking Clock. Thus any indication of British Summer Time to the nearest second is not to be trusted.
Jim Hositees, Suffolk.

QUESTION: Do universities fiddle their exam results?

☐ IN 1951 I was a temporary employee at Senate House, London University. My job was to go through examination papers to make sure that only the allowed number of answers had been marked and the marks had been properly totalled. In one paper, fewer than the usual number of candidates had passed, so we had to go through and add five marks to each paper. Is this 'fiddling'?
Hilda Handoll, Prestatyn, Clwyd.

☐ IT DEPENDS on what is meant by fiddling. Marking inevitably is subjective. To an extent this can be minimised by having papers set and/or read by more than one examiner. In North American universities, where classes are often larger, continuous evaluation and frequent testing play a larger role than in this country, and marking may be by student teaching assistants. Some academics, in pursuit of objectivity and on the questionable assumption that there is a normal distribution of student ability which recurs from year to year, may award grades in predetermined proportions, viz. 15 per cent firsts, 35 per cent seconds, 35 per cent thirds and 15 per cent failures, commonly modified by 'marking to a curve', with marks plotted on a graph and the actual division into classes determined by the occurrence of so-called 'natural breaks' in the distribution along the curve. In Canadian universities, perhaps reflecting stronger residual British influences, these pernicious approaches are less common than in the US. A mitigating factor is that the examinations system in both Canada and the US is more open than is usual in British universities. Students are told the actual mark obtained, have their scripts returned, can compare these with their fellows, may discuss their answers with their examiner, who normally will be their lecturer, and

even argue against marks awarded for individual questions, and, finally, may request a formal review.
Jack Thirgood, Professor Emeritus, University of British Columbia, Canada.

QUESTION: Have any of the inventions demonstrated on *Tomorrow's World* ever become a huge success?

☐ I THINK the fax speak for themselves.
(Dr) Frances Szekely, Chatteris, Cambs.

☐ YES! The home computer, the compact disc, the Phone-card, the CAT scanner, the pocket calculator, the personal stereo, the disposable camera, the portable telephone. The list goes on and on. And *Tomorrow's World* was also the first to show you . . . 'suspenderless stockings'. The name may have been lost in the mists of time but the invention wasn't. Tights.
Dana Purvis, Editor, Tomorrow's World, *BBC Television, London W14.*

☐ INMARSAT-C, a satellite communications system for people on the move, was demonstrated on *Tomorrow's World* in June 1990 and has since become a global success. More than 2,000 small, battery-operated Inmarsat-C terminals are being used by journalists and business travellers and on trucks and ships, to send and receive messages from any-where to anywhere in the world. Médecins sans Frontières, the medical aid team, has used it to distribute supplies, as has Unicef, in areas of Africa, Latin America and the Middle East, where the nearest telephone or telex machine was hundreds of miles away.
Bhawani Shankar, Inmarsat, London NW1.

QUESTION: Why do doors on trains in Britain open outwards?

☐ AS A commuter I find the outward-opening doors particularly useful for dispersing the boarding crowd that gathers around the door when I am trying to alight.
(Ms) S. Head, Gosforth, Newcastle upon Tyne.

QUESTION: Instead of wishing one another 'Good luck' or 'Break a leg' on first nights, opera singers say 'Toi toi'. Why?

☐ BOTH 'Break a leg' and 'Toi toi' are of Central European origin and based on folkloric superstitions. 'Break a leg' is simply a translation of the German 'Hals und Beinbruch' (literally: '[Wishing you] neck-and-leg fracture') – but why should such a calamity serve as a good wish? It seems that we are dealing here with an attempt to outwit Fate: since it is assumed to bring us, in its cussedness, the opposite of what's being asked of it, what could be simpler than this 'double bluff' – request something bad, and out of sheer contrariness Dame Fortune will present you with something good. 'Toi toi' is simply a phonetic rendering of spitting, believed to be a powerful antidote to malign influences (including the Evil Eye). In both cases there is clearly a suggestion of belief in magic, some of it no doubt quite ancient.
C. P. Carter, Richmond, Surrey.

QUESTION: Why does jelly wobble?

☐ IT WOBBLES because of its underlying molecular structure and the way this is built up. Jellies are usually made from gelatin, extracted from animal bones (although special quick-setting types can also be made from seaweed extracts). When gelatin molecules are warmed in water they are the shape of long wriggling worms, but when the solution

is cooled some of these individual molecules become inter-
twined with one another to form bits of triple helix, and the
net result is to form a still bigger molecule, which also
becomes branched like a tree. Eventually, as this process
continues, the result is that some of these new 'supermolecules' are so big that they span from one side of the jelly to
the other and form a three-dimensional 'net' stretched
across the material. This is elastic, because if one side of the
sample is pushed or knocked, the energy in the movement
can be carried right across the jelly via these supermolecules
to the other side, causing it to wobble. If the jelly is then
reheated the helical strands become unwound and the jelly
melts. Actually the mechanical behaviour of jellies is not so
different from that of a car tyre, which is also made up of
gigantic 'cross-linked' rubber molecules, but luckily the
links for these are more permanent, otherwise driving in hot
weather would be hazardous.
*(Prof.) S. Ross-Murphy, Biomolecular Sciences, King's Col-
lege, London.*

☐ PROFESSOR Ross-Murphy gets a gamma minus for answering only half the question. The problem is familiar to
the engineer who designs large buildings to resist earthquakes. Try this. The first ingredient is elasticity, the property of a body to recover from deformation. Push the jelly
with a spoon and release it. It recovers its original shape,
whereas the cream does not. The second ingredient is resonance. Take a ball or a weight and suspend it from your
hand by a length of rubber (linked rubber bands will do).
Explore the dynamic properties of this elastic system as
follows. Beat time with your hand. At slow time the ball
follows the hand; at faster time it moves further than the
hand, and at faster time still there seems an almost unlimited tendency for the ball to increase its oscillation. This
is the condition of resonance: the ball and rubber band are
acting as an amplifier of the hand's motion. The jelly acts

similarly, magnifying the tiny motions of the table as it shakes under the movements of the people sitting round it. Try putting the dish on a thick cloth laid on a concrete floor. The jelly becomes static (unless you live near a busy road or railway).
R. T. Rose, Warrington, Cheshire.

QUESTION: Why is a pirate flag called the Jolly Roger?

☐ THE Pembrokeshire pirate Bartholomew Roberts, known as Barti Dhu or Black Barti, had as his personal flag a skeleton on a black background. Other pirates liked the design and copied it. Barti wore a red coat and the French nicknamed him 'Le Joli Rouge', which was corrupted into 'Jolly Roger' and came to mean the flag rather than the person. Barti was a rather strait-laced sort of pirate who banned drinking on board ship, insisted on early nights for the crew and never attacked on a Sunday. He was killed in an encounter with a Royal Navy ship in 1722, aged 40. Yours with a yo-ho-ho and a bottle of rum.
Diana Salmon, Llanfyrnach, Dyfed.

☐ YO HO . . . er, hang on a bit. May I contradict Ms Salmon? The Jolly Roger, or Skull-and-Crossbones, was first used by a French pirate, Emmanuel Wynne, about 1700.
J. Claydon, Newmarket, Suffolk.

☐ ANOTHER possibility is that English pirates in the Indian Ocean began to refer to the red flag of the Tamil pirate Ali Raja by his name and 'Ally Roger' or 'Olly Roger' was later corrupted to Jolly Roger. The English word 'roger', meaning a vagabond rogue, may be another explanation. David Mitchell, in his book *Pirates*, discusses this question and seems to prefer a derivation from Old Roger – a synonym for the Devil.
Graham Hulme, Leicester.

QUESTION: Why does my phone go 'ting' very quietly about midnight?

☐ EACH night a computer at your local exchange tests all the lines. When this happens, just enough current is passed down the line to make your phone go 'ting'. Only phones with a 'real bell' are affected by the test. Light sleepers should change their phone for the 'warbler' type or ask BT to stop testing their line.
Gerry Simpson, S. Croydon, Surrey.

QUESTION: Two bottles of wine on the table, one white, one red; one label says 'Mis en bouteille', the other 'Mise en bouteilles'. What Gallic subtlety (if any) am I missing?

☐ THE Gallic subtlety concerns a point of grammar and has nothing to do with the colour of the wine. 'Mis en bouteille' has *mis* as a past participle used adjectivally, meaning 'put in a bottle'. *Mis* is masculine because it agrees with *le vin*. 'Mise en bouteilles' is a substantive form of the verb *mettre*, meaning 'the bottling process'. The noun formed from the verb is *la mise* and clearly the bottling process needs lots of bottles, which is why *bouteilles* is in the plural.
Helen Winnifrith, Leamington Spa, Warwicks.

QUESTION: Who were the Situationists?

☐ THEY believed in the Society of the Spectacle, as defined in Guy Debord's book of the same name. The book, over which no copyright is held or rights reserved, contains 221 paragraphs or statements which define the spectacle society. Reading too many paragraphs at one sitting can make your brain melt and run out of your ear. Here is an example. Paragraph 3: 'The spectacle presents itself simultaneously

as all of society, as part of a society, and as instrument of unification. As a part of society it is specifically the sector which concentrates all gazing and all consciousness. Due to the very fact that this sector is separate, it is the common ground of the deceived gaze and of false consciousness, and the unification it achieves is nothing but an official language of generalised separation.'
Kevin Rickis, Edinburgh.

☐ 'ABOLISH work!'; 'Under the paving stones, the beach!'; 'Run for it – the old world is behind you!' These slogans capture the revolutionary spirit of the Situationists. The Situationist International (SI) was a politically extreme movement, formed in 1957 out of the Lettrist International, the International Movement for an Imagist Bauhaus, and the London Psychogeographical Society. Although never numbering more than 70, the Paris-based group had a wide influence in artistic and avant-garde circles before disbanding in 1972. Drawing on Hegel and the early Marx, and the traditions of Dada and Surrealism, they sought to confront the image-saturated world of late capitalism. However, the SI broke from received ideologies and refused categorisation, attacking most parties, organisations and leftist gurus. Alienation was now total, they believed, with everyone being passive onlookers in the Society of the Spectacle. Even opposition was repackaged and sold back to us, recuperated by the ruling elite. They pursued a total critique of everyday life and aimed to transform urban spaces through spontaneous, playful and creative revolt. The SI split in 1962, with the artistic wing regrouping in Scandinavia. The remaining Situationists concentrated on spreading their theories, slogans and notoriety through underground networks and public scandals, reaching a climax in the riots and occupations of Paris in 1968. Soon afterwards, the SI's last three members dispersed. Their ideas first fed into the mainstream through punk. In the last few years, their fame has spread, with their work being simplified and often

depoliticised by exhibitions, TV shows, magazine articles and potted histories such as this.
David Pinder, Robinson College, Cambridge.

□ SHOULD the questioner wish to partake of the Spectacle, he will find the *Situationist International Anthology* available at Frontline Books in Manchester. Having read the work, however, I doubt that the irony experienced will compensate for the £10.50 surrendered.
John Green, Altrincham, Cheshire.

□ AS ALWAYS when the Situationist International is discussed (see above), the errors, half-truths and misunderstandings proliferate. The Situationists didn't fade away like old soldiers after 1968. For example, in 1975 a book called *A True Report on the Last Chance to Save Capitalism in Italy*, ostensibly written by a conservative elder statesman using the pseudonym 'Censor', became the subject of enthusiastic reviews and fascinated speculation in the Italian press. 'Censor' was congratulated by parliamentarians, bankers and journalists for his lucid analysis of the social crisis that had beset Italy since the 'hot autumn' of 1969. Eventually the Situationist Gianfranco Sanguinetti revealed himself as the author. In March 1984, Gerard Lebovici, the publisher of Guy Debord's books and other Situationist material, was mysteriously assassinated in Paris. The French press unleashed a hysterical campaign, heaping slanders on Lebovici and presenting Debord as his 'bad angel', as a terrorist, a Russian agent and much else besides. Debord responded in a brilliantly written little book, *Reflections on the Assassination of Gerard Lebovici*. Those seriously interested in the SI should make their way to the bookshop at the premises of Editions Gerard Lebovici (27 rue Saint-Sulpice, Paris), where they'll find a lot of good reasons for improving their French.
J. Bonnot, Belfast.

QUESTION: Which language is easiest to learn?

☐ ALL languages are approximately equally easy for a child learning a first language. The ease with which an adult may learn a second language depends to some extent on how similar the new language is to that person's first language. For example, German and Dutch share a good deal of their vocabulary and grammar rules, making each one relatively easy for speakers of the other to learn. By this criterion alone, Frisian, Swedish, Danish or Norwegian should be candidates for the easiest second language for an English native speaker. Opportunity and motivation are also factors. It will be easier to learn French in a French village, where it is essential for daily life, than in England in a mainly English environment. Respect for a language and its speakers will remove psychological barriers to learning – so ease of learning is also relative to a social context. Resources at the learner's disposal (teachers, their methods and the available support materials) may outweigh the factors mentioned above in determining how readily a second language is learned, and of course they have nothing to do with the nature of the language itself. Pidgin and Creole are relatively easy languages to learn. These are created by adults who already have a first language, in a situation where there is no common language already available and no opportunity for formal learning. They have relatively small vocabularies and a minimum of grammatical rules. New Guinea Pidgin, now called Tok Pisin, is the national language of Papua New Guinea. Most of its vocabulary derives from English but it still requires an active effort to learn. The English, Spanish and French Creoles of the Caribbean and elsewhere originated as pidgin languages. Although often the object of scorn from the unenlightened, some of these languages have a literary tradition and daily newspapers printed in them, and/ or have been used as a medium of education. In social terms these have been more successful than the many

attempts to create 'easy-to-learn' artificial languages for international communication.
Mark Sebba, Lecturer in Linguistics, Lancaster University.

QUESTION: As moths are attracted by artificial light at night, why are they not drawn by the light of the moon?

☐ MOTHS were on Earth millions of years before Man arrived (and with him artificial light). The only bright light visible at night was the moon, and it is by this that moths navigate: by keeping the moon at a fixed angle, a straight line of flight is maintained. So when a moth encounters an artificial light at night, it mistakes it for the moon and, in an effort to maintain a constant angle, continually overcompensates for the apparent deviation from its flight-path and spirals into the light.
Phil McGhee, HM Prison Glenochil, Tullibody, Clacks.

QUESTION: It is a much quoted maxim that there are only seven stories in fiction and that all others are based on them. Is it true, and what might these seven stories be?

☐ IF IT *is* true, do you think someone should introduce Barbara Cartland to the other six?
Jim McNeil, Sheffield, S. Yorks.

☐ I'M NOT sure about plots for stories, but plots for plays is something my father, the Irish playwright Denis Johnston, had a lot to say about. Originally he thought there were seven, but then he realised there are in fact eight:
1. Cinderella – or unrecognised virtue at last recognised. It's the same story as the Tortoise and the Hare. Cinderella doesn't have to be a girl, nor does it even have to be a love

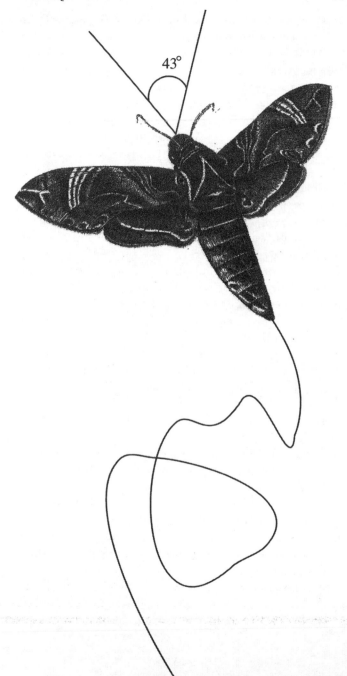

story. What is essential is that the Good is despised, but is recognised in the end, something that we all want to believe.

2. Achilles – the Fatal Flaw that is the groundwork for practically all classical tragedy, although it can be made comedy too, as in the old standard Aldwych farce. Lennox Robinson's *The Whiteheaded Boy* is the Fatal Flaw in reverse.

3. Faust – the Debt that Must be Paid, the fate that catches up with all of us sooner or later. This is found in all its purity as the chase in O'Neill's *The Emperor Jones*. And in a completely different mood, what else is *The Cherry Orchard*?

4. Tristan – that standard triangular plot of two women and one man, or two men and one woman. *The Constant Nymph* or almost any French farce.

5. Circe – the Spider and the Fly. *Othello*. *The Barretts of Wimpole Street* if you want to change the sex. And if you don't believe me about *Othello* (the real plot of which is not the triangle and only incidentally jealousy) try casting it with a good Desdemona but a poor Iago.

6. Romeo and Juliet – Boy meets Girl, Boy loses Girl, Boy either finds or does not find Girl – it doesn't matter which.

7. Orpheus – The Gift taken Away. This may take two forms: either the tragedy of the loss itself, as in *Juno and the Paycock*, or it may be about the search that follows the loss, as in *Jason and the Golden Fleece*.

8. The Hero Who Cannot Be Kept Down. The best example of this is that splendid play *Harvey*, made into a film with James Stewart.

These plots can be presented in so many different forms – tragedy, comedy, farce, whodunnit – and they can be inverted, but they still form the basis of all good writing. The fault with many contemporary plays is simply that they do not have a plot.

Rory Johnston, London NW3.

□ RORY Johnston's listing of eight basic plots for plays

seems very inadequate. Georges Polti, in his famous book
The Thirty-Six Dramatic Situations, classified these not by
legendary/mythological tales of archetypes or personalities
(Faust, Circe, etc.) but by the situation itself, e.g., no. 10,
'Abduction'; no. 25, 'Adultery'; no. 3, 'Crime Pursued by
Vengeance', etc., etc. Nobody to my knowledge has
improved on Polti's 36 possible plots, though some of his
sub-divisions taken from classical models are, to say the
least, tenuous (Situation 26e: 'A woman enamoured of a
bull'). Confusion may have arisen with the old saying among
comedians that there are only seven basic jokes.
John Pilkington, Playwright, Exeter, Devon.

☐ TO MR JOHNSTON'S eight plots for plays you can add
David and Goliath – the individual against the repressive/
corrupt powers of the state or community, or their rival
claims. As in *Enemy of the People*, *The Visit* and, of course,
Antigone.
Leslie Caplan, London NW3.

☐ CONSIDER the following application of Mr Johnston's eight
prototypical plots:
1. Cinderella. Rick, an expat Yank bar-owner in wartime
Morocco, begins as a drunken cynic but his 'essential good-
ness' is at last celebrated.
2. Achilles. Like the Greek warrior, the proud, 'fatally
flawed' Rick – once a doer of great deeds – spends most of
the story sulking in his tent. He is forced into selfless action
only for the sake of the refugee Elsa, the woman he loves.
3. Faust. Rick's good looks, fame and wealth may be
parochial but they are Faustian and gratuitous. Inevitably,
Rick's debt is called in and he gives up his business, his girl
and everything he has lived for.
4. Tristan. Manly Rick (Tristan) loves and is loved by sultry
Elsa (Isolde) but she is already married to wimpish Victor
Lazlo (King Mark).
5. Circe. Elsa's wiles entice Rick into her service only to
destroy him.

6. Romeo and Juliet. Once, in Paris, Rick and Elsa loved and lost each other. Here, in Morocco, they get back together but are finally parted again.

7. In a concrete sense the gift taken away is a Letter of Transit which would enable Rick to go back to America but which he is forced to give up to Lazlo. More symbolically, the gift is of personal happiness and is sacrificed to political necessity, since to save Lazlo is to save the world for democracy.

8. The Irrepressible Hero is Rick personified.

There is also a ninth archetypical story-line, the Wandering Jew, which is bafflingly excluded from Mr Johnston's list. Rick is, of course, the persecuted traveller who will never return home. Thus, instead of eight (or nine) stories, there is only one, and it is called *Casablanca*.

Robin Blake, London WC1.

□ THERE are only about seven themes in fiction, and they include Love, Money, Power, Revenge, Survival, Glory and Self-awareness. It is the quest for these that makes a story. Most stories have more than one theme and it is the superimposition of themes, with the arising conflicts, that makes a story interesting. Robin Blake's suggestion that all stories can be imposed on the *Casablanca* plot is really saying that *Casablanca* contains several basic themes, which it does, most of which are not resolved and in general are badly written. Nevertheless, the film is good because of its dramatic tension, partly created by the fact that actors were given their scripts on a daily basis, so never knew the ending themselves. It might also have been quite a different film if the original actor chosen for the lead had played the part: Ronald Reagan.

Stan Hayward, Author of Scriptwriting for Animation, *London NW2.*

QUESTION: What is the origin of the three brass

monkeys with hands covering eyes, ears and mouth? Are these the same as the monkeys that suffer in cold weather?

☐ I THINK they originate in Japan. In the Tosho-gu shrine in Nikko, built in the seventeenth century, the three monkeys are one of a series of eight carvings, meant to exemplify ideal behaviour on the part of children – they should see, speak and hear no evil, for example.
Edward Curran, London SE27.

☐ IT SEEMS likely that the three monkeys (*sanbikizaru*) do have a Japanese origin, since they are in fact a Japanese pun. The word for 'monkey' (*saru* or *zaru*) is homophonous with the negative verb ending *zaru*. It is therefore a fairly obvious play on words to represent the slogan *mizaru, kikazaru, iwazaru* ('see nothing, hear nothing, say nothing') by means of three monkeys in appropriate attitudes – just as you might, if you wished, represent the English 'catastrophic, catagmatic, catalytic' by means of three cats. The word *mizaru* ('see nothing') can also mean 'three monkeys'.
G. H. Healey, School of East Asian Studies, Sheffield University.

☐ THE 'suffering' of brass monkeys in cold weather has nothing to do with the castration of primates. In the days of sailing ships, men-o'-war carried cannon-balls in pyramidal heaps on the gun deck. They were prevented from rolling about by having the bottom layer enclosed in a triangular frame (like an enlarged version of the frame used to set up the balls at the start of a snooker game) which was made of brass and known to sailors as a 'monkey'. This arrangement was very stable against all but the most violent pitching and rolling, except in cold weather. Then, the brass monkey (since it had a greater coefficient of expansion than the cast-iron cannon-balls) would shrink relative to the bottom row of balls and thrust them upward. Beyond a certain point this

would put the centre of gravity of each bottom ball too high for stability. Hence the expression 'Cold enough to freeze the balls off a brass monkey'.
D. E. M. Price, Handsworth, Birmingham.

☐ MR PRICE'S explanation of the cold-weather problems of these primates is ingenious but unconvincing. Over the relevant range of temperatures, the differential contraction of a brass trivet versus a pyramid of cast-iron cannon-balls is unlikely to amount to more than fractions of a millimetre. While it might just be possible with modern manufacturing techniques to replicate the effect described under laboratory conditions, it seems highly unlikely that the builders of men-o'-war were capable of manufacturing to such fine tolerances as to reliably cause the phenomenon your correspondent described.
Gavin C. Bell, Aberdeen.

☐ THE myth of 'brass monkeys' aboard sailing warships has no basis in reality. In 20 years of research into men-of-war, I have found absolutely no contemporary evidence for their existence. In fact, cannon-balls were carried in wooden racks fitted to the sides of the ship beside the guns. In 1780 an order was issued by the Navy Board to replace these with holes drilled in the coamings (the raised timbers round the hatchways). Since this would have cost practically nothing, it is very difficult to see why anyone would think of using an expensive material such as brass; especially since, according to the myth, it was not very effective in cold weather. Brass ought to survive under water much better than wood or iron, yet I have never heard of anything like a 'brass monkey' being recovered from a shipwreck.
Brian Lavery, Assistant Curator (Naval Technology), the Historic Dockyard, Chatham, Kent.

QUESTION: Who invented 'fizzy' drinks?

☐ IT WAS the Reverend Dr Joseph Priestley (1733–1804), who announced his discovery in his 'Directions for impregnating water with fixed air; in order to communicate to it the peculiar spirit and virtues of Pyrmont water, and other mineral waters of a similer [*sic*] nature', published in 1772 and dedicated to the Earl of Sandwich (who also made his contribution to the fast food industry).
Peter Grant, Rare Books Dept, Sanders of Oxford.

QUESTION: How long is a piece of string?

☐ IT'S this long.
H. MacLean, Easdale, Argyll.

☐ I REMEMBER reading in an Arabian Nights book way back in the Thirties of a certain Caliph of Baghdad who would give his daughter to any man of wealth who could answer three questions correctly. Failure, of course, meant an early departure from the mortal coil. One crafty prince decided that a visit to the King of the Underworld was in order, not trusting the Caliph to play a straight bat. His Satanic Majesty was happy to oblige for the usual fee (the prince's soul). Two of the questions were: 'How long is a piece of string?' and 'How deep is the ocean?' The answer to the first is 'From end to end' and the second 'One stone's throw'. The third question eludes me. Incidentally, the prince won his princess but had problems with Satan later on.
W. L. Gange, Carnforth, Lancs.

☐ I DON'T know, but the *Guardian* reported on 2 October that under the new schools curriculum seven-year-olds would be required to 'find a quarter of a piece of string'.
Marion Sweeney, Caerphilly, Mid Glam.

☐ I HAVE waited with some interest for a serious answer to this question but have so far been disappointed; it raises important issues. Firstly, there are questions to be answered about the determinacy of the boundaries of objects. Secondly, there are questions about the relative accuracy of different measuring instruments and methods. Thirdly, it raises profound questions about the fundamental nature of the universe, i.e. wave versus particle explanations, and the Einsteinian concepts of time and the effect of relative movement. Could someone with the appropriate qualifications be bold enough to venture the answers which I do not feel qualified to give?

Tony Faulkner, Rochester, Kent.

QUESTION: Are slugs edible?

☐ AT UNIVERSITY in Bristol, I shared a house with a veterinary student who had a propensity for consuming unpleasant foodstuffs while under the influence of alcohol. On one occasion he spooned large quantities of margarine directly from the tub into his mouth. This does not compare with the incident which took place outside a public house in mid-Wales. His sister picked up an enormous black slug, proclaiming 'Isn't it beautiful! I can see its eyes.' Inexplicably, this induced my flatmate to take hold of the slug and swallow it whole. By the time he returned home he was consumed with guilt, having realised the grave consequences of his actions for the well-being of the slug. In an attempt to induce vomiting, thereby giving it a slim chance of survival, he drank copious quantities of dirty washing-up water, to no avail. Since my friend felt no ill-effects, I suppose it could be concluded that slugs are indeed edible.

Piers Sadler, London N5.

☐ IN ABOUT 1938 a young friend told me that his uncle had to eat live slugs as a treatment for tuberculosis. These were swallowed whole after being dipped in golden syrup to make

them palatable. This was, presumably, a homoeopathic treatment.
Philip Langford, Bristol.

☐ I HAVE eaten the whitey-grey ones at a special camp for Scouts. We put them in salt water and then boiled them. They can be served with or without butter. Chewy but tasteless.
Peter Jennison (aged 12), Shipley, W. Yorks.

☐ IN THE book *A Country Calendar and Other Writings*, by Flora Thompson (edited by Margaret Lane, OUP, 1979), the following story appears under the entry for December: 'It is quite probable that no one need starve while there are slugs and snails to be found and a fire is forthcoming to cook them by. In a certain village in the Midlands . . . a poor woman with a large family was suspected of receiving stolen mutton, because . . . her children were the plumpest and rosiest in the parish. The authorities searched her cottage and found a barrel of meaty morsels salted down in her larder. This at first was taken for finely minced mutton but, upon examination, proved to be slugs which she had gathered in wet weather to provide all the meat her children were likely to taste.'
(Mrs) L. B. Pankhurst, Ashford, Kent.

☐ THE story quoted by Mrs Pankhurst has a certain charm but is unlikely to be true. Putting salt on slugs results in a slimy goo; hardly any chance of a 'barrel of meaty morsels salted down', I would have thought.
Roy Lee-Faulkner, Stalybridge, Cheshire.

QUESTION: Since when has the standing ovation been a ritual of party conferences? Who holds the record?

☐ THE late Joseph Stalin enjoyed standing ovations lasting

up to an hour. The reason was that nobody wanted to be seen to be the first to sit down.
David Walsh, Skelton, Cleveland.

☐ THE record for the largest number of standing ovations at a party conference, and probably also the longest ovation, must go to Nicolae Ceauşescu, the late Romanian leader. At a party conference in November 1989, he made a speech condemning the changes in Eastern Europe, warning against them happening in Romania and recalling the effective measures employed against them in China. All delegates rose and Ceauşescu was given no less than 67 consecutive standing ovations. Within six weeks the security forces had been beaten, Ceauşescu was dead and the party had more or less ceased to exist.
Bruce Dickinson, Bristol.

QUESTION: 'Pass the sick bag, Alice.' Who was Alice?

☐ WASN'T Alice the dreaded disease that Christopher Robin went down with?
Gordon Roberts, Formby, Liverpool.

☐ SHE was a canteen lady at the old Express building in Fleet Street. Part of her job was to deliver meals for hard-pressed journalists to eat at their desks. On Saturdays, when she bore plates of steaming eggs and chips to the back bench of the *Sunday Express*, Sir John Junor, who naturally ate at the Savoy Grill, used to look disdainfully at them and utter the immortal words.
Roger Watkins, Ingrave, Essex.

QUESTION: How do food companies work out the number of calories in their products?

□ THE calorific content is measured with a device known as the bomb calorimeter. A sample of food is placed in an airtight chamber – the 'bomb' – which is filled with pure oxygen and then placed in a tank of water. The food is ignited by an electric spark so it completely burns up. The temperature increase in the water is measured and the actual energy content of the food can then be calculated, either in old-fashioned calories or more modern joules. This method is not completely accurate, as it is rather crude when compared to the way the human body uses food. For example, proteins are completely burned up in the bomb calorimeter, whereas in the human body some of them would be used not for energy but for the production of things like skin, hair, mucus and muscle tissue. Incidentally, the subject is well covered in most biology textbooks for A-level and above, as well as in the occasional Open University programme on television.
Daniel Foster, Breaston, Derbyshire.

□ THE four sources of food energy – protein, fat, carbohydrate and alcohol – yield 4, 9, 3.75 and 7 calories per gram respectively. The calorie value of a food is usually estimated by multiplying the protein, fat, carbohydrate and alcohol content by the appropriate factors. Many food manufacturers do not carry out chemical analyses but instead estimate the calorie content using values for ingredients derived from tables published by HMSO. Such calculations are normally within 10 per cent of the actual value.
(Dr) Tom Sanders, King's College, University of London.

QUESTION: What is the origin of the silent 'w' before 'r' in English words such as 'wrap', 'write', 'wring' etc.?

□ THE retention of the silent 'w' is useful in distinguishing between homonyms: 'write'/'rite'; 'wrote'/'rote'.
David Keogh, Bray, Co. Wicklow.

☐ DAVID Keogh's argument for the retention of the obsolete 'w' to distinguish between 'write' and 'rite', 'wrote' and 'rote' is flawed because these words show their difference easily through context and grammatical function, i.e. verb/noun. This kind of objection to spelling reform is spurious. *Adrian Murphy, London SE16.*

☐ BEFORE the seventeenth century the 'w' was pronounced. Other letters ('g' in 'gnaw' and 'k' in 'knee', for example) fell silent too, but were trapped in the spelling as written English fossilised into its present form. They are all of ancient Germanic origin and were pronounced in Anglo-Saxon. German, which is generally spelt as spoken, writes *reissen* (cognate with 'write') without the original 'w' and *nagen* (cognate with 'gnaw') without the original 'g', but has kept the 'k' in *knie* because it is pronounced. Other letters fell silent in English before they could be fossilised, and so disappeared. Anglo-Saxon spelt 'loaf', 'neck' and 'rough' with an initial 'h' as 'hlaf', 'hnecca' and 'hrioh', but it was dropped around the thirteenth century when no longer pronounced . If that 'h' had been pronounced a few centuries longer, we would no doubt write 'hloaf', 'hneck' and 'hrough' today. The 'wh' words lie in between. Anglo-Saxon wrote 'when' and 'white' as 'hwenne' and 'hwite', and some accents (e.g. Scots) still say 'hw'. Later 'hw' was reversed to match 'ch', 'gh', 'sh' and 'th'. There is currently great concern about literacy but little improvement is possible until our spelling is defossilised, and such absurdities as 'wr', 'gn' and 'kn' reduced to the letters we actually speak. The Simplified Spelling Society is campaigning for English spelling to be modernised (secretary: Bob Brown, 39 Chepstow Rise, Croydon CRO 5LX. Tel: 081-686 3793). *Christopher Upward, Editor-in-Chief, Simplified Spelling Society, Birmingham 14.*

QUESTION: Is it possible to cook fish in a dishwasher?

☐ I FEEL certain that I saw Vincent Price, the horror film actor, cooking a trout in a dishwasher on *The Simon Dee Show* in the Sixties. The fish is sealed in a foil parcel after being seasoned, given a squeeze of lemon juice and garnished with parsley. Care should be taken to ensure the foil wrapping is impervious to water, otherwise the natural juices produced by the fish in cooking will be lost. Cooking time will vary from machine to machine but usually the longest wash cycle will suffice. Needless to say, addition of detergent and rinse additive does nothing to enhance the flavour.

David Chapman, London W7.

☐ AN UNPROTECTED fillet caught up in the high-pressure jets of a dishwasher would disintegrate. Whole fish are likely to fare better than their boned brethren but if they are in close proximity to a spray arm nozzle (water pressure 0.25 bar) they are likely to find their internals forced out through the eye sockets; this might be construed as a benefit. Wrapping a fish in foil – *à la* boil-in-the-bag – should ensure survival but the best prospect would surely be to put it in a watertight ceramic container with a little water and effectively steam-cook the blighter. However, since water temperatures in a dishwasher maximise at around 70°C, this is a dubious proposition. Above all else, cooking a fish in a dishwasher would be very wasteful: you would use many litres of water and a relatively large amount of electricity. And if things went wrong you would invalidate any manufacturer's guarantee. A slightly less daft idea is to use a top-loading washing machine to cook bulk quantities of rice. (The rice is put into a pillow case and the water temperature switched to a maximum 95°C.) The result is said to be 'very fluffy' – thanks to the effect of the water agitator. However, the machine ends up clogged with starch, and again you lose your guarantee.

Gerry Hinde, Deputy Editor, Independent Electrical Retailer, *West Liss, Hants.*

QUESTION: Was St Augustine black?

☐ THIS story stems from the fact that the saint (born 354 AD) was a native of the Roman province of Africa, which covered roughly the same area as modern Tunisia (the Romans called the continent Libya). The Roman Empire was a little like the Soviet Union, each province having both a distinctly local population and a fair mix of citizens from throughout the Empire. However, it is quite likely that Augustine was a true native. Most of the cities in Africa had been founded before the Romans arrived by Phoenicians from Lebanon, while the rural population were closely related to modern Berbers. As to Augustine's appearance, we might, perhaps, imagine him to have borne some resemblance to that latter-day ideologue, our own dear Colonel Gaddafi.
Alex Woolf, Dept of Archaeology, University of Sheffield.

QUESTION: An advertisement for a new kind of gel-filled hot 'water' bottle states: 'According to figures published by the DTI for 1987, over 80 per cent of reported accidents involving hot water bottles were scalds or burns caused by boiling water.' What were the other 20 per cent?

☐ MY PATERNAL grandmother died on 6 August 1970, as a result of injuries sustained when a hot water bottle (full) fell 15 floors from a tower block in Hulme, Manchester, hitting her directly on the head. She was from Sverdlovsk, USSR.
(Mr) Beart Sry, Caton, Lancs.

☐ DURING the dark winter nights of 1986, in a bitter marital argument over 'quilt-nicking', I was clouted viciously by my first wife with a hot water bottle. I cannot say if this incident was recorded by the DTI.
Peter Good, Brighouse, W. Yorks.

☐ I PRESUME the data quoted was taken from the DTI's Home Accident Surveillance System (HASS). The remaining 20 per cent were mainly falls, the majority of which involved tripping over the hot water bottle.
Helen Pedley, Consumer Safety Unit, DTI, London SW1.

QUESTION: How many countries are there in the world?

☐ IT ALL depends on how you define a country. The requirement used for the list below is that it should be generally recognised as independent, i.e. responsible for all its own affairs. Unfortunately there are some anomalies. Scotland cannot reasonably qualify, even though it is allowed separate teams at the Commonwealth Games and the soccer World Cup. Bophuthatswana is also out (recognised by South Africa but nobody else), as are all accepted colonies. The Order of the Knights of Malta is apparently recognised as a sovereign entity by some 40 countries but is not included. Taiwan is in − clearly independent though not universally recognised. Also in are the Vatican, Monaco, Liechtenstein and other places (though their independence must be in doubt because of their size and geographic or political situation). The result is: Afghanistan, Albania, Algeria, Angola, Antigua and Barbuda, Argentina, Australia, Austria, the Bahamas, Bahrain, Bangladesh, Barbados, Belgium, Belize, Benin, Bhutan, Bolivia, Botswana, Brazil, Brunei, Bulgaria, Burkina Faso, Burundi, Cambodia, Cameroon, Canada, Cape Verde, Central African Republic, Chad, Chile, China, Colombia, the Comoros, the Congo, Costa Rica, Cuba, Cyprus, Czechoslovakia, Denmark, Djibouti, Dominica, the Dominican Republic, Ecuador, Egypt, El Salvador, Equatorial Guinea, Ethiopia, Fiji, Finland, France, Gabon, the Gambia, Germany, Ghana, Greece, Grenada, Guatemala, Guinea, Guinea-Bissau, Guyana, Haiti, Honduras, Hungary, Iceland, India, Indonesia, Iran,

Iraq, Ireland, Israel, Italy, the Ivory Coast, Jamaica, Japan, Jordan, Kenya, Karibati, North Korea, South Korea, Kuwait, Laos, Lebanon, Lesotho, Liberia, Libya, Liechtenstein, Luxembourg, Madagascar, Malawi, Malaysia, Maldives, Mali, Malta, North Mariana Islands, Marshall Islands, Mauritania, Mauritius, Mexico, Micronesia, Monaco, Mongolia, Morocco, Mozambique, Myanmar, Namibia, Nauru, Nepal, the Netherlands, New Zealand, Nicaragua, Niger, Nigeria, Norway, Oman, Pakistan, Palau, Panama, Papua New Guinea, Paraguay, Peru, the Philippines, Poland, Portugal, Qatar, Romania, Rwanda, St Lucia, San Marino, São Tomé and Principe, Saudi Arabia, Senegal, Seychelles, Sierra Leone, Singapore, Solomon Islands, Somalia, South Africa, Spain, Sri Lanka, Sudan, Surinam, Swaziland, Sweden, Switzerland, Syria, Taiwan, Tanzania, Thailand, Togo, Tonga, Trinidad and Tobago, Tunisia, Turkey, Tuvalu, Uganda, USSR, UK, United Arab Emirates, USA, Uruguay, Vanuatu, Vatican City, Venezuela, Vietnam, Western Samoa, Republic of Yemen, Yugoslavia, Zaïre, Zambia, Zimbabwe. Total: 170 countries.
Tom Marlow, Saffron Walden, Essex.

☐ IF, as Tom Marlow suggests, the definition of a country is that it should be 'responsible for all its own affairs', then several of the countries in his list have to be removed. Britain retains the oversight (and therefore the control) of the defence policies of Antigua and Barbuda, the Bahamas, Barbados, Dominica, Grenada, St Lucia, and Trinidad and Tobago. The United States is responsible for the foreign and defence policies of the North Mariana Islands, the Marshall Islands, Micronesia and Palau (and won't surrender control until Palau abandons its nuclear-free constitution). Deleting these countries reduces the total from 170 to 159.
Joseph Nicholas, London N15.

☐ TOM Marlow's list omits St Kitts and Nevis and St Vincent

and the Grenadines (both members of the United Nations),
and Andorra.
Neil Grosvenor, Wolverhampton.

☐ TOM Marlow's list omits Eritrea, whose independence
from Ethiopia was finally granted in July 1991, after 30
years of struggle.
Roger West, London SW8.

☐ IN THE 'International Calls' section of my current phone
book, 212 countries are listed (excluding the ship's telephone service). In the national section I reckon there are
seven countries: UK, Irish Republic, Isle of Man, Jersey,
Guernsey, Alderney and Sark. These add up to 219. This
listing implies no view whatsoever of sovereignty or status
but it is one way of dividing up the world.
Gregg Coulson, Belfast.

☐ MAY I offer a round-up now that further comments seem
to have come to an end? One correspondent suggested that
membership of the United Nations is a sign of independence.
I note that Byelorussia and the Ukraine have each been
members of the UN in their own right since 1945 but clearly
do not yet qualify. Another reader wished to exclude various
West Indian and Pacific territories because of their remaining connections to the former imperial power. If this is right
then there are others to exclude; for example I believe that
the foreign affairs of Monaco are handled by France. And
the UK has given up some sovereignty to the European
Community, so is it also off the list? Andorra should have
been in – my error. St Kitts and Nevis and St Vincent and
the Grenadines have detached from the UK and should be in
but I am now convinced that the North Mariana Islands
should not be included, mainly because their inhabitants
are ultimately to become US citizens. This does not apply
to the Marshall Islands, Micronesia and Palau, which all
have a lesser association with the US. Estonia, Latvia and

Lithuania seem now to qualify (the USSR has agreed that they are independent) and Eritrea can probably be added. All this makes the current total 176.
Tom Marlow, Saffron Walden, Essex.

QUESTION: Why do flies congregate around centrally hung light fittings, even when the light is not on?

☐ FLIES congregate where other flies have congregated. Their favourite places are marked by collections of brown spots about half a millimetre in diameter and are not restricted to light fittings, but if a light does attract flies this will initiate a 24-hour parking place. No doubt they are attracted by the parking markers put down by previous occupants. It's just like the scars along country roads which lack a lay-by.
(Sir) James Beament, Queens' College, Cambridge.

QUESTION: I wish to be buried at sea. How can I arrange this?

☐ THE main requirements are a weighted coffin with plenty of holes drilled in it, a boat whose captain is not superstitious about carrying dead bodies, and a licence from the Ministry of Agriculture, Fisheries and Food. This last may seem surprising but is a stipulation of the unromantically titled Dumping at Sea Act 1974. When you think about it, there is good reason for the fisheries authorities to exercise some control over the place of sea burial. There are companies who advertise themselves as specialists in this area but any good funeral director should be able to arrange it. Unless you happen to die on a world cruise, it is usually more expensive to be buried at sea than it is to be cremated or buried in the earth. We advise those who are nautically

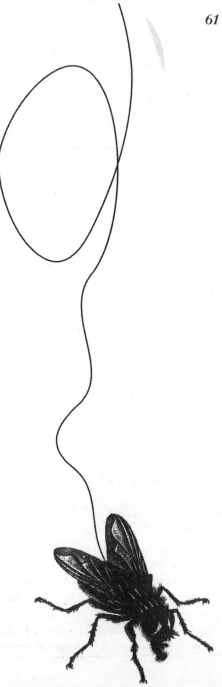

minded to go for cremation and have their ashes scattered on
the briny deep.
Graham Williams, Chosen Heritage Ltd, East Grinstead, W.
Sussex.

**QUESTION: Despite many years' service in the British
Army (infantry), I am unable to answer a friend's question as to why the names of British tanks all start with
the letter 'C' (Cromwell, Chieftain, Churchill, Challenger, etc.). Can anybody help?**

□ IN 1921 the British Army decided to classify its weaponry
into four broad categories. Tanks were given a 'C' categorisation and, during several military exercises which followed,
this letter was actually painted on to the participating
tanks. It wasn't long before tank crew members began scraw-
ling nicknames on their vehicles as a continuation to this
initial letter ('Cockalilly' was one such famous example).
In the subtle way that institutions often have of stamping
out a practice by absorbing it, the Army Department
responded by giving names (rather than numbers) to their
new generation of tanks and ensuring that each name
began with a 'C'. The innovation soon became an established
tradition.
Lt.-Col. R. G. Duffield (retd), ex-14th Armed Lancers and
Lineshooters, Tunbridge Wells, Kent.

□ AT THE beginning of the Second World War, the British
Army had A9 Valentines and A13 Matildas, both of which
were designated as infantry tanks, i.e. fairly heavily
armoured but not very fast. From 1941 onwards, the need
was for faster, lighter tanks designated as 'cruisers', especially for the North African desert fighting. These included
Crusader, Covenanter and later the Cromwell, followed
by its larger version, the Comet. I suggest the names came
from being classed as 'cruiser' tanks and also from the

Christie suspension around which they were designed. (The Churchill did not fall into this category but its name seemed highly appropriate at the time.) The post-war Chieftain and Challenger, though classed as battle tanks, have simply followed an established tradition of names.
Harvey Quilliam, Liverpool 13.

☐ I SERVED seven years in the Royal Tank Regiment and came across various explanations, including the fact that the Armoured Vehicles Research and Development Establishment was at Chertsey. I was even told that the first tanks taken into action in the First World War were manned by crews from the 3rd Battalion of the Tank Corps, 'C' being the third letter of the alphabet.
John D. Shaw, Liverpool 13.

QUESTION: When football supporters sing 'You'll never walk alone' on the terraces, are they in breach of Rodgers's and Hammerstein's copyright?

☐ THE song is a fully copyright work and any unauthorised use, performance or recording constitutes an infringement. In practice, all football stadia and other places of entertainment, and radio and TV stations, hold 'blanket' licences from the Performing Rights Society which cover such performances. If the football version is recorded on tape, video, etc., it attracts the normal mechanical copyright royalties. Chappell's were the British publishers of this song when Liverpool fans began to chant it following a pop recording by Gerry and the Pacemakers. I recall that Richard Rodgers was puzzled, amused and rather flattered by its adoption.
Len Thorpe, Warner Chappell Music Ltd, London W1.

QUESTION: Who decides that a person is important

enough to use the VIP lounge at Heathrow airport and what are the criteria?

☐ THE Foreign and Commonwealth Office, in conjunction with the Department of Transport, draws up a list of people entitled to use VIP suites at airports in the UK. At Heathrow this includes members of royal families, heads of state, government ministers and leaders of opposition parties represented in Parliament. As you can imagine, it is not easy to get added to the list.
Mike Roberts, Acting Managing Director, BAA Heathrow, Hounslow, Middx.

QUESTION: What happens to a cow if you don't milk it?

☐ IF MILK is not removed pressure builds up which eventually stops the secretion so that no more milk is produced. If the cow is producing very little (less than 5 kg/day) when milking stops there are no problems; this is the normal way of 'drying off'. If the cow has recently calved and is producing a lot of milk then the pressure would be exceedingly uncomfortable and infection could occur.
(Dr) D. J. Roberts, Senior Specialist, Grassland and Ruminant Science Dept, The Scottish Agricultural College, Dumfries.

QUESTION: Boxers, wrestlers, etc., are classed according to weight to avoid giving anyone an unfair advantage. Why are there no classifications in sports where height is crucial (e.g. basketball)?

☐ THE questioner is right that none of the major professional basketball leagues has height classifications. However, it is common in the US for there to be certain leagues that operate an 'under 6 ft' or 'under 6 ft 4 in' rule for players. In addition, many players would disagree that height is crucial. In the American professional league one player is 5 ft 3 in tall and another 5 ft 7 in. They clearly demonstrate that the sport can be played at the highest level by 'small' people. The situation becomes more complicated when you consider that the more important physical aspect in basketball is 'reach', not height (people's arms vary in length). Similarly, jumping ability, speed, etc., are all very important. The answer, therefore, is that height is not − most of the time − considered crucial enough.

Mark Rodgers, Kidlington, Oxford.

QUESTION: The Cynics were a sect started in ancient Greece by Diogenes. Why were they called Cynics instead of Diogenics?

☐ DIOGENES was not the founder of the Cynic sect but merely the best-known member of it. The Cynics traced their origin to Antistheses, one of Socrates' companions, and thence to Socrates himself. Cynic doctrine emphasised that individual virtue and happiness could be attained only by a rejection of the world and its conventions and this was exemplified in the way of life followed by members of the school. It was apparently because of their uninhibited 'natural' behaviour that the Cynics acquired their name, which is equivalent to the Greek word for 'dog', an epithet applied to them by those outraged by Cynic immodesty. Diogenes seems to have accepted this nickname with equanimity, and, according to a contemporary account, a marble dog was placed over his grave. Presumably the modern meaning of 'cynic' has developed from the Greek Cynics' tendency to distrust outward show and to attempt to dispel men's illusions wherever possible.

Michael Rendell, Poole, Dorset.

QUESTION: Is it true that a black hole hit Siberia early this century?

□ ON THE morning of 30 June 1908, a large object, either a comet or, more probably, a meteor, passed over central Siberia. At a height estimated to have been between 5 km and 8.5 km above ground level, the object exploded. The resultant fireball caused atmospheric disturbances which were detected around the globe. The district most affected by the explosion, in the drainage basin of the Podkamennya Tungushka river, was heavily forested and sparsely populated. The first scientific expedition to the area, in 1921, discovered that trees had been blown down more than 40 km from the central area. Dry timber had been ignited by thermal radiation up to 15 km from the central area. No crater has been found, suggesting complete fragmentation of the object in the upper atmosphere. Since black holes are, well, black and eyewitnesses described the object which caused the 'Tungushka event' as very bright, the answer is probably no.

David Robertson BSc, Dept of Earth Sciences, Liverpool University.

□ THERE have been many theories about the explosion near the Tunguska River in June 1908. Evidence from the site shows an explosion of enormous magnitude, up to 1,500 times that of Hiroshima. Trees were spontaneously ignited at a distance of 10 miles. Some 1,200 square miles of forest were flattened by the blast, which was recorded in London as traversing the globe twice. Other reports from the area of black rain, grey blisters on livestock, clouds glowing at night and people dying of 'invisible fire' were not recorded again until 37 years later in Japan. The meteor/comet theory is difficult to justify in front of such evidence, coupled with the lack of any sizeable crater. This has led to the belief of an 'air burst' of some other object. That the source of the blast was nuclear in origin is likely, but accounting for an explosion

rivalling a large H-bomb in Siberia in 1908 is difficult, to say the least.
Paul Green, Shanklin, Isle of Wight.

☐ THAT the cataclysmic explosion in the Tunguska region of Siberia was nuclear in origin seems unlikely. The most probable explanation is that a comet ploughed into the atmosphere and immolated itself at an altitude of about five miles. In the area affected by the blast, a high concentration of tektites (materials normally found in objects from outside the Earth's lithosphere) confirms that whatever exploded was indeed from outer space. Not that this proves what the object actually was. One theory suggests that our planet was sucked into a doughnut shape as a black hole passed through it. Given that the Earth's plate tectonics would have been drastically altered, and the disturbance caused at the other side as the black hole came out again would have been colossal (just as a bullet makes a neat hole on the way in, and anything but on the way out), this admittedly seductive theory is full of holes. My favourite postulation comes from the fact that the object – described as cylindrical in shape – was seen in one area travelling at a significantly different angle to that mentioned by those viewing it from further north. This led to the suggestion that it was in fact being steered – a spacecraft which was trying to take on water at Lake Baikal but went out of control. QED: it was a joyrider. The phenomenon of 'daylight' in Britain, which occurred for the next couple of nights, is explained by the amount of dust excavated by the blast, which diffracted the Sun's light around much of the globe to areas where it should have been dark. Someone managed to play a round of golf at St Andrews at 2.30 in the morning. Newspapers concluded that this was the work of the aurora borealis, dismissing reports of a huge explosion as frivolous. One thing previous correspondents have failed to mention is that it could happen again, any time, anywhere. Sleep tight!
Alan Kidd, Folkestone, Kent.

QUESTION: We are, respectively, 5 ft 10 in and 6 ft 4 in tall. If we stand shoulder to shoulder on the beach, is there a significant difference in the distance of the horizon we can both see?

□ THE Earth is more or less a sphere and you are both standing on its surface. This can be represented as follows: Where r is the radius of the Earth, d is the height of eye of any person standing on its surface. The horizon is the distance x from the eyes to the point where a tangent is formed with the Earth. Angle ABO is a right angle. By Pythagoras, $x=(r+d)\ r$. That gives x as the square root of $(d+2rd)$. Treating the eye height as the actual height, and assuming that the radius of the Earth is 3819.72 miles, x is the square root of $(70+2\times70\times3819.72\times1760\times36)$, or 2.905 miles for the individual who is 5 ft 10 in. For the one who is 6 ft 4 in the distance is 3.027 miles, giving a difference between the two of about 214 yards.
Jim Betts, Shipley, W. Yorks.

□ THANKS to Jim Betts, I now know why the formula I've used for years works. I found it in W. W. Sawyer's *Mathematician's Delight* (published by Pelican). Sawyer says: distance (in miles) = the square root of 1.5 times height (in feet) above sea level. This gives a result which, for practical purposes, is close enough to Jim Betts' calculation and — more to the point — can be done on the back of a beermat. From Sawyer's formula we can derive the height above sea level needed to be able to see, say, the Isle of Man from the Lake District: height = $\text{distance}^2/1.5$ or $0.667\times\text{distance}^2$.
Michael Furey, Rotherham, S. Yorks.

□ THE distance also depends on the latitude at which the observer is standing, and on the direction of his or her gaze. The Earth is not a perfect sphere since its radius at the poles is some 21 km less than that at the Equator. Standing at the North or South Pole, looking towards the Equator, the

shorter of the two observers will see a distance of 4,636.28 m, while his taller companion will see 4,842.92 m, a difference of 206.64 m. If, however, the two observers prefer to compare their horizons in warmer climates, standing on the Equator, looking towards the poles, then the difference shrinks to 204.08 m. The difference increases to 205.55 m if the observers turn their gaze to the east or west. All of which goes to prove that taller people are more far-sighted than the rest of us.
David F. Hadley BSc, Dept of Geology, University of Liverpool.

☐ THE answers so far leave out the fact that the line of sight to the horizon will be affected by atmospheric aberration, rendering any difference indistinguishable to the human eye.
Gordon Joly, London E14.

QUESTION: The idea of shipwrecked mariners sending messages in bottles has become a cliché. Are there any documented examples of this resulting in rescue?

☐ ON 17 January 1876, an Austrian merchant ship was wrecked off the Atlantic islands of St Kilda. Nine crewmen were given hospitality by the islanders who were themselves in danger of starving owing to the severity of the winter. The sailors and islanders combined to launch two SOS vessels to take advantage of the Gulf Stream currents and inform the mainland of their joint distress. These 'vessels', containing a bottled message, were little canoes hewn out of log and attached to an inflated sheep's stomach. One vessel reached Orkney within nine days; the other reached Poolewe in Wester Ross within 22 days. HMS *Jackal* was despatched to St Kilda and took the shipwrecked Austrians to the mainland. (Source: Tom Steel, *The Life and Death of St Kilda*, Fontana.)
Hector Urquhart, Loughborough, Leics.

QUESTION: Why is it traditional to stand on a soap-box to get your point across? Why not a fruit box, for instance?

☐ IF YOU stood on a fruit box people might think you were a nut case.
Madeleine Cox, Mansfield, Notts.

☐ IN THE nineteenth century soap was distributed to shops in strong wooden boxes. Candles were the only other common domestic commodity distributed in this way, so it was a toss-up whether orators stood on soap or candle boxes. Other dry goods, such as sugar and beans, came in sacks. Fruit came from the country in baskets and punnets until the invention, between the wars, of shallow stacking boxes made of plywood. But these are too low and weak to replace the traditional soapbox for speeches, even though cardboard and staples had by then made the real thing obsolete.
Laurie Smith, Carshalton, Surrey.

QUESTION: What did ploughmen really eat for lunch?

☐ EDWIN Grey, in his book *Cottage Life in a Hertfordshire Village*, concerning the period 1872–1922, describes the food of farm workers (including ploughmen). An easily got-together meal consisted of bread and cheese, a raw onion and a pint of beer. He also described meat dumplings containing flank of beef, streaky bacon, pickled pork or liver and flare (?), with onion or parsley, heated over a gypsy fire. Grey did not remember any complaints of indigestion, though he did hear the effects of wind. In addition, bloaters were cooked over a fire in newspaper or toasted 'as the Gypoes do'. One man exclaimed, as his fish burst open at the throat, 'My bloater's abeginning ter git a bit warm, 'e's undone 'is shirt collar'. Besides beer, cold tea was taken for

refreshment. The food was carried on the back in baskets woven from plaited rush. Can anyone explain what 'flare' is? *Brian Palmer, St Albans, Herts.*

☐ FLARE (or flead) is the fatty membrane found around the kidneys and loin of the pig, and is the porcine equivalent of beef suet, providing the fat in the dumpling Mr Palmer mentions. When rendered, it gives the best-quality lard, but when pigs were raised and slaughtered at home, pastry was made by beating flare directly into the flour. 'Flead cake' was made by adding sugar and spice to the basic mixture. *Dafydd Roberts, London N1.*

☐ IN Worcestershire in the early years of this century, a ploughman's lunch was not his mid-day meal (his dinner), which was eaten at home, but his mid-morning snack, often known as 'bate'. It was eaten afield and there was an established procedure, requiring dexterity arising from long practice. The left hand held the food: a thick slice of bread between the thumb and first finger, a hunk of cheese between the first and second finger, and a slippery onion between either second and third, or third and fourth (whichever was most comfortable). A clasp knife in the right hand cut a slice from each in turn, and in strict order, the onion topping the bread and cheese. All this was washed down by home-brewed cider (supplied by the master), carried in a stone jar encased in wicker. Again, the dexterity was marked. The heavy jar was swung up to the mouth by a finger thrust through the lug, the cork often extracted by the teeth, and, head back, the worker sank a mighty draught. *Evelyn Ward, Rhiwbina, Cardiff.*

QUESTION: When using a Walkman, which is the greater drain on batteries: allowing the tape to play to the end or fast-forwarding?

□ AS A film sound recordist, I have to carry my own spare batteries, so I am keen to keep battery drain to a minimum. Some years ago I measured and compared the current used in playing to the end, fast-forwarding and rewinding. The current used at fast-winding speeds is not proportional to the speed, but much less, partly because the tape is no longer pressed against the heads but can move smoothly. The electronics are usually still alive and taking current as well even though they are not being used. Therefore the most important factor is the time taken to play or wind the cassette. Take a worst-case cheapo Walkman look-alike and assume the fast-forward speed is only 10 times faster than playing. Also, as a worst case, if the current drain is three times greater while winding forward, there is a saving of at least three-and-a-bit times by fast-forwarding. In practice, the saving on a faster machine can be as great as 10 or 15 times, simply due to the shorter time taken.
Dave Brinicombe, BBC Film Unit, London W5.

QUESTION: In a TV commercial for ice cream, mashed potatoes were once substituted for the real thing because it melted under the lights. Is this still done?

□ I HAVE only once used coloured mashed potato to simulate scooped ice cream. This worked for a medium shot but was not really acceptable in extreme close-up. It is better to photograph the real thing under as few hot lights as possible. Ice creams like Walls Cornetto never look perfect when you take them out of their packaging, so we make perfect models of these. An interesting use of models is for shots simulating molten chocolate pouring into a mould to form a chocolate bar. Many different models are made and shot in stop-frame to create the illusion of pouring. I am told that baked beans are usually all model beans and only the sauce that goes over them is real. Provided the photographed result looks like the

real thing I find this type of food photography quite acceptable.
Arnold Pearce, London NW3.

☐ A FRIEND of mine once appeared in a commercial for anti-dandruff shampoo. He didn't actually suffer from it so a bar of white soap was grated into his hair to simulate the affliction. It was then brushed out to appear, miraculously, dandruff free.
J. Coles, London SE1.

☐ ANYONE interested in some of the other tricks, such as swapping engine oil for syrup and so on, should read *Everything You Always Suspected Was True About Advertising But Were Too Legal, Decent and Honest to Ask*, by Martyn Forrester.
Keneth Dillon, Kilmalcolm, Renfrewshire.

QUESTION: In the wartime song, Vera Lynn sings of 'bluebirds over the white cliffs of Dover'. Why bluebirds? These warblers are native to America and would never be seen near Dover.

☐ THE bluebirds of North and Central America feature in many American popular songs from the Twenties onwards, signifying happiness and well-being. Titles include 'Bluebirds in the Moonlight' (from the film *Gulliver's Travels*), 'Bluebird Sing Me a Song', 'Bluebird of Happiness', etc. The American writers of 'White Cliffs of Dover' (Walter Kent and Nat Burton) were probably unaware that there are no bluebirds as such in England. Incidentally, Walter Kent had not seen the cliffs of Dover until he made a special visit a couple of years ago – nearly 50 years after writing the song.
Len Thorpe, Warner Chappell Music Ltd, London W1.

☐ THREE subtle messages are apparent in the one line of this

song: (i) American bluebirds a
can pilots flying from English ai
a sky-blue underside, and (iii
synonymous with the RAF unif
message is: 'whatever happe
flying'.
Tim Heyes, Treuddyn, Clwyd.

QUESTION: A significant per
is red–green colour-blind.
colours become accepted as

□ COLOURED light signals gov
transport systems were introdu
before the characteristics of d
appreciated. The advantage of
high-intensity signals can be
glass filters. These colours came
most people in daylight and a
men (one in 12) and 0.5 per c
have some form of red–green
different types of deficiency and
in each type. Only about 3 per
distinguishing bright reds and
cannot see red lights at all afte
such as those used for domest
blue and green/yellow stripe in
blue/green in the USA) can
deficient people but are unsuita
ling at night. Red for 'danger' o
or 'go' are accepted world-wid
but to exclude colour-deficient
making a mistake, from key
interpretation might endanger
Jennifer Birch, Colour Vision
London EC1.

ce and provide a special
tters, a few punctuation
ar, the size of 10 regular
minute and no breaks, we
urs before the word 'To'
owing) comes into view.
would require another 12
' would warrant a lot of
rth, not to mention around
in the process. A fraction
lay, would require 'more
le world' (John 21:25), as
uts it. Thus, for practical

ommunity Medicine, Cam-

the unusual benefit of a
for each letter of the
te the beast hits these keys
ate of one per second. And
ate task is to type the word
s a one-in-27 chance of
tap: relatively quick and
ible two-letter sequences:
by 'A' with one second
(according to the laws of
seconds. 'MAC' is one of
nces; and 19,683 seconds
seconds. If one continues
grows, it will be found that
in probability, not be
31 years before the word
accident. Of course, a
ck could do the job in just

dy, Manchester.

☐ IT ALL depends on what you mean by 'really feasible'. Given an infinite amount of time anything that could happen will happen. The complete works of Shakespeare produced by a typewriter-toting chimpanzee is such a possibility, i.e. it is not logically self-contradictory. Whether an infinite amount of time is 'really feasible' is the crunch question. The problem thus is not to do with the chimpanzee but with the lifespan of the universe. If the universe lasts for ever, the chimpanzee will make it. My bet is that it won't, because it isn't.
(Dr) William Johnson, Arnside, Cumbria.

☐ I HAVE had this problem with apes before. As soon as they learn to type a 12-line essay, such as 'How I Spent My Summer Holiday', they think they are God's gift to literature. Before you can say 'Twelfth Night', they are off looking for something better. Those who show any real promise may make it to Hollywood as scriptwriters, where they will find there is no shortage of people prepared to slap them on the back and hand them a banana daiquiri. After a while the novelty wears off and the decline is normally rapid – from hack writer to bit parts in Tarzan films, then skid row.
Murray Allison, London N8.

☐ ALL the answers so far assume that the only restriction is the amount of time available. But ribbons and typewriters wear out, trees have to be cut down to make paper, chimps have to be fed. So unlimited resources would be needed. One thing cosmologists seem to be agreed on is that the amount of matter in the universe is finite (the great astrophysicist Arthur Eddington reckoned that it contained only 10 raised to the power of 79 protons), so even with infinite time the odds against stochastic Shakespeare are even longer than those calculated by your correspondents.
S. K. Epton, Whitby, S. Wirral.

☐ THE chimpanzee must be understood as an example of randomness and the complete works of Shakespeare as an example of an enormous number of symbols of 27 different types (the letters of the alphabet plus the space bar for separating words) arranged in a specific order. Knowing how long it would take to type just one word even if working at a good speed, and knowing that the chimp will succeed in typing the complete works of Shakespeare (because given that amount of time it is necessarily so), we realise that infinity is a concept quite difficult to understand. So the answer is: of course it is feasible, but as long as you think of the chimpanzee as not being a real one and the same with the typewriter and the paper it uses. It's only a way of picturing an abstract idea.

Alex Guardiet, Fulwood, Sheffield.

☐ THE complete works of Shakespeare would never occur by chance. The chimpanzee is faced with 27 keys and may press any of them. Therefore, all letters (and the space bar) would have an equal chance of being selected and in any large sample each would occur approximately the same number of times. Absolute equality would be approached more and more closely as the amount of typing increased. The letters comprising the complete works of Shakespeare are far from a random selection. In English the letters 'A', 'D', 'E', 'I', 'N', 'O', 'R', 'S' and 'T' occur far more frequently than 'J', 'K', 'Q', 'V', 'X' and 'Z'. It would be impossible for a chimpanzee to produce a lengthy, random sequence of letters that reflected this inequality. One might expect the letters towards the centre of the keyboard to be hit more frequently than those towards the ends. However, this possibility does not improve the chances of the works of Shakespeare being typed by chance. On a standard 'Qwerty' keyboard, 'A' occurs to the extreme left, whereas 'J' and 'V' are near the middle.

Gregory Beecroft, Welwyn Garden City, Herts.

☐ GREGORY Beecroft appears to have been hitting a few random keys himself when he claims that the complete works 'would never occur by chance' because the letters of the alphabet are not equally frequent in English but are hit with equal probability by the chimpanzee. Even if two events – say the typing of a 'Z' and the typing of an 'E' – are equally probable, this does not necessarily mean they will occur equally often in a given random sequence. Similarly, there is no guarantee that any sequence of tosses of an unbiased coin will produce equal (or even approximately equal) numbers of heads and tails. A thousand consecutive heads, although exceedingly unlikely, is not an impossibility with a fair coin; neither is Shakespeare with a chimpanzee. The letter frequencies used by Shakespeare are irrelevant. Any pre-specified sequence of letters is just as likely to occur as any other, regardless of its composition. Thus a sequence consisting entirely of 'Z's is no more or less likely to be produced than any other given sequence (including Shakespeare's works). Even if Shakespeare's works consisted entirely of 'zzzzzzzzzzzzzz . . .' (*A Midsummer Night's Dream*, perhaps?) the chimp's chances would not have changed.

Ben Craven, Stirling.

☐ DISREGARDING practical considerations such as typewriter wear and the expiry of the universe, and assuming the chimp continues to press the keys at random, Mr Guardiet claims it will 'necessarily' produce a copy of the works of Shakespeare and Mr Beecroft that it will never achieve the feat. Both are wrong. In an infinitely long random series of typewriter symbols you can expect any finite string of such symbols – whether a short one such as 'to be' or a longer one such as Shakespeare's complete works – to occur an infinite number of times. In this case, Shakespeare's works should appear just as often in the ape's typescript as any given string of the same length containing unusual letters of the

alphabet in the same proportion as common ones. However, there remains a tiny chance that the string sought will never occur. Infinite number theory gives fascinating results and it is hard to illustrate how small this chance is. If you imagine enough eternally typing chimps to completely fill a Newtonian universe of infinite size then you would still need more before probability favoured one of them omitting the works of Shakespeare from its script.
Graham Haigh, Milnthorpe, Cumbria.

☐ SCANDALOUSLY, the literary implications have hardly been considered by previous correspondents. In order to produce one 'complete works' the chimp would first have to produce, in addition to millions of pages of complete garbage, thousands of incomplete works (it would also be certain to pass through several minor poets on the way). If it were possible to do it at all, then it should be possible to improve on the original. Some of the many variant versions would be free of all sexism, racism and militarism. That would indeed be a complete edition of Shakespeare.
Gabriel Chanan.

☐ PERHAPS if the problem involved a monkey producing the complete works of Jeffrey Archer people would find it easier to believe that the feat would, unfortunately, be achieved.
M. J. Moody, Beeston, Notts.

☐ I AM currently engaged in trials with some chimpanzees to find out whether, given an inexhaustible supply of materials, they can produce a nuclear missile.
A. P. Eines, Southbourne, Dorset.

QUESTION: At the beginning of Len Deighton's latest novel, *Spy Sinker*, the following sentence appears: 'The

author asserts the moral right to be identified as the author of this work.' What does this mean?

☐ IT REFERS to a new provision under the Copyright, Designs and Patents Act 1988. I can do no better than quote from an excellent article, 'British Copyright Law', by Amanda L. Michaels, published in the *Writers' and Artists' Yearbook 1990*: 'Another new departure in the Act is the provision of "moral rights", commonly known as the rights of "paternity" and "integrity". The right of "paternity" is for the author of a copyright literary, dramatic, musical or artistic work, and the director of a copyright film, to be identified as the author/director in a number of different situations, largely whenever the work is published, performed or otherwise commercially exploited' (Section 77). 'However, the right does not arise unless it has been "asserted" by the author or director, by appropriate words in an assignment, or otherwise by an instrument in writing' (Section 78) . . . Writers should therefore aim to ensure that all copies of their works carry clear assertions of their rights under this provision. 'The right of "integrity" is not to have one's work subjected to "derogatory treatment". This is defined as meaning an addition to, deletion from, alteration to, or adaptation of a work (save for a translation of a literary or dramatic work) which amounts to a distortion or mutilation of the work or is otherwise prejudicial to the honour or reputation of the author/director.'
Linden Stafford, Skipton, Yorks.

QUESTION: I once read that the stance of a horse in an equestrian statue indicates how its rider died. Can anyone provide more information?

☐ THE theory – horse rearing on hind legs, rider killed outright in battle; horse with three legs touching ground, rider died of wounds sustained in battle; all four legs on ground, rider survived battle – is complete nonsense and there is no iconography of horses' hooves. This is quickly proved by choosing an equestrian statue, e.g. the notoriously bad one of Field-Marshal Haig in Whitehall, checking the hooves and finding out how the rider died. Haig's round-about-style charger has one hoof off the pedestal, although the Field-Marshal did not die of wounds. Note that many military commanders who rode horses in battle do not get a horse in their statue because it massively increases the cost of the statue and most of them were paid for by public subscription.

Ralph Lloyd-Jones, London SE22.

☐ RALPH Lloyd-Jones is wrong to dismiss this as non-sense. It is certainly true of many equestrian statues on the Civil War battlefield of Gettysburg – now a national monument – which I was fortunate enough to visit in the company of historians from the military college nearby.

Vivian Green, Lightwater, Surrey.

QUESTION: Why do we laugh when we are tickled by others, but not when we tickle ourselves?

☐ TICKLING is not a DIY experience. It takes two to tickle. Indeed, thinking about tickling, it is usually associated with the erogenous zones – areas of the body associated with vulnerability and steeped in primitive fears. You always know when a tickle is coming because there is a blend of two emotions – fear and pleasure. Certainly it is unhealthy to tickle yourself. Finally, the zones of tickling can be pierced and invaded, but it has to be pointed out that no one has ever been stabbed in the soles of the feet!

Ken Dodd, Knotty Ash.

QUESTION: Has anyone ever died of boredom?

☐ ON THE face of it, George Sanders, the suave film actor, would seem a likely candidate. When in 1972 he did away with himself with a lethal cocktail of Nembutal and vodka, the most publicised of his three suicide notes declared: 'Dear World. I am leaving because I am bored. I feel I have lived long enough. I am leaving you with your worries in this sweet cesspool. Good luck.' But Sanders had been suffering for some time from a screwed up private life, feelings of rootlessness, severe financial problems and deteriorating health. The give-away word is 'cesspool'. However stylish the form of his farewell note, 'boredom' is scarcely the word to summarise his sad decline. Since chronic boredom is closely linked with depression − is, in fact, a form of depression − it's doubtful that anyone ever died of boredom in the relatively trivial everyday sense of the word. However, when human beings are subjected to solitary confinement and sensory deprivation, they are often brought to the brink of despair and self-destruction.
Neil Hornick, London NW11.

☐ DEAN W. R. Inge was accurate in his contention (see *The End of an Age*, 1948) that: 'The effect of boredom on a large scale in history is underestimated. It is a main cause of revolutions . . .' The answer has to be yes, lots.
(Rev.) Clifford Warren, Machen Rectory, Gwent.

☐ BOREDOM has certainly been responsible for a number of deaths, often by mistake. Louis XIV regularly started wars out of sheer boredom. In Chicago in 1923 Nathan Leopold and Michael Loeb plotted the murder of a schoolboy, just as a relief for their interminable ennui. Death has also been caused in trivial moments of tedium: on 2 November 1973, a passenger was killed on a DC10 because an engine exploded after a bored flight engineer had meddled with a

few of the buttons in the cockpit. Although Samuel Beckett's two tramps in *Waiting For Godot* might be suffering a terminal boredom when they whine 'we are bored to death', and Nasa is worried that it may well cause serious problems on the manned mission to Mars, it's unlikely that boredom leads to the final decision to die rather than continue a life of bland indifference. In the words of Morrissey, that guru of bedsit boredom: 'I think about life and I think about death, but neither one particularly appeals to me.'
John Dutton and Chris Horrocks, London N4.

□ MY FAMILY is convinced that an actor cousin, who died sadly while in the cast of *The Mousetrap*, must indeed have died of boredom.
S. Marking, Toller Whelme, Dorset.

□ ON 31 July 1861, whichever of the Goncourt brothers was on *Journal* duty that day asked whether their lack of success might actually mean they were failures. He then adds: 'One thing reassures me as to our value: the boredom that afflicts us. It is the hallmark of quality in modern men. Chateau-briand died of it, long before his death. Byron was stillborn with it.'
Richard Boston, Reading, Berks.

QUESTION: Why do athletes have to race around the track in an anti-clockwise direction?

□ PERHAPS they are running against the clock?
R. A. Cotmore, Mansfield, Notts.

□ BECAUSE of the effect of the Earth's rotation, an athlete running anti-clockwise will have a slight advantage, result-ing in a faster time. In the Southern Hemisphere, this effect is reversed but, as the sport grew up in the Northern Hemisphere, anti-clockwise races have remained, despite the international status of athletics. Evidence of this phenomenon is that none of the current world track records has been set south of the Equator. The question is, if the World Championships are ever held in the Southern Hemisphere, would the IAAF decide that track events should be run in the opposite direction?

Peter Brown, Sheffield.

☐ THE answer involving gravitational effects was not convincing. I think the tradition goes back to the Olympic Games, *circa* 700 BC. The ancient Hippodrome appears to be based on an anti-clockwise race with competitors coming up to the finishing line at the end of the straight (see the booklet *Olympia, Altis and Museum*, by Nikolaos Yalouris, Verlag Schnell and Steiner München; Zurich Art Editions, Meletzis and Papadakis, Athens). Later, in Rome, the chariot races in the Circus Maximus must also have been anti-clockwise. The Circus was overlooked by the emperors on the Palatine Hill, so the finishing line was on the eastern side of the north, where the *spina* ended (see the model of ancient Rome in the Museo della Civiltà Romana). Perhaps an expert can confirm my speculation?

G. G. Bernard, Gillingham, Dorset.

☐ NOW that chariot races have been mentioned, is it not possibly due to the predominant right-handedness of our species? Overtaking with a long whip in the right hand would be less likely to cause havoc by whipping the wrong horse (or rider)!

Roger Franklin, Stroud, Glos.

☐ ON AVERAGE athletes have stronger right legs, while horses, though leading with the left foreleg, exert greater power through the right hind leg than the left, so it is rational to require the stronger legs to cover the greater distance. This is why both infantry and cavalry commanders

have always preferred, if possible, to execute encircling tactics in an anti-clockwise direction.
John Veale, Woodeaton, Oxford.

☐ THE ancient Greeks may have run anti-clockwise round their stadia, but it is a mistake to assume that the tradition was unbroken until modern times. Contemporary illustrations show that when running on tracks was revived in the nineteenth century, clockwise running was probably just as common. Oxford and Cambridge universities ran clockwise – Oxford until 1948, Cambridge until some time later. The first modern Olympic Games in Athens (1896 and 1906) and Paris (1900) used the clockwise direction, but in 1906 there were complaints, as many countries had by then settled for the anti-clockwise practice. From 1908 the Games have all been run 'left hand inside'.
Peter Lovesey, Bradford-on-Avon, Wilts.

QUESTION: Why do TV weatherpeople never cast a shadow behind them, even though they are strongly lit from the front?

☐ THERE is no shadow behind the weatherpeople because there is no real picture behind them. What the camera sees is the presenter standing in front of a plain blue screen. The presenter is lit from the front and the side, and the plain blue screen is lit from behind, which cancels out any shadows. The map you see on the screen at home is projected onto the blue space electronically. The map itself has been produced on a computer graphics terminal and, using a vision mixer in the control gallery, the map is superimposed over any blue areas – in this case, the special blank blue screen – so it appears that the presenter is standing in front of the map. You'll notice presenters never wear anything blue, because if they did the map magically would appear here, too.
Sally Galsworthy, Itnl Weather Productions Ltd, London NW1.

QUESTION: Why do we put the clocks back two months before the shortest day (21 December) and not put them forward again until three months after?

☐ THERE does not seem to be any scientific reason for doing this. Time is not fixed in nature. Man has fixed time. At the end of October, the sunrise time is approximately 06.44 GMT; the sunset time is approximately 16.44 GMT. By the end of January the sunset time is already back to 16.44 GMT, yet sunrise time is still only 07.37 GMT. Sunrise time does not compare to October until the end of February. It does appear that the decision of our legislators to extend winter time by four weeks until the end of March is an arbitrary one.
Andy Wright, Brighton.

☐ I BELIEVE this was brought about by the Defence of the Realm Act. This allowed the Government to create laws quickly and easily to help the war effort. It was deployed in the First or Second World War (I am not sure which) to ensure that everyone put their clocks back one hour in winter, thus gaining an hour of worktime towards the war effort.
S. R. Emmanuel, London SW6.

QUESTION: I have heard that in the Wild West the practice of scalping was introduced by European invaders, not the native American Indians. Is there any evidence, one way or the other?

☐ IT IS thought that scalping existed among some of the eastern tribes of North America before the arrival of settlers. But wherever it originated, scalping was encouraged and spread to different tribes by the Spanish, English, French and Dutch, who offered bounties for the scalps of their enemies. Kit Carson condoned scalping in his war against the Navajo (who believed it a barbaric Spanish practice). In

1863, the state of Minnesota paid $25 for each Sioux scalp and Colonel Chivington, responsible for the Sand Creek massacre, advocated the scalping of all 'indians', including children.
Simon Leigh, Survival International, London W2.

☐ SCALPING is not unique to North America; it is mentioned by Herodotus and Procopius as occurring in the Ancient World. Different cultures bring back evidence of a kill in different ways, such as cutting off ears or other easily removed bits. The Good Book provides some hideous examples. Taking scalps is no better or worse than using a Gatling gun on women and children, or giving them cholera-infected blankets.
Ralph Lloyd-Jones, London SE22.

QUESTION: Given the pre-eminent status of the sees of Canterbury and York, why were our ancient universities founded in Oxford and Cambridge and not in these medieval cities?

☐ OUR ancient universities were not founded: they seem to have grown up spontaneously. Nobody there wanted archbishops breathing down their necks, interfering with academic freedom or the students' fun. It was the same in other countries: Paris, not Rheims, became the seat of France's most prestigious university; Bologna and Padua, not Rome, the seat of Italy's. Oxford did get a bishop at the Reformation, and his relations with the university were not always easy. 'I do not love thee, Dr Fell,' probably represented the feelings of quite a few Oxford people towards their bishop. T. H. Huxley won friends in the university by his demolition of Bishop Wilberforce, and even Bishop Gore in the twentieth century found that Oxford was a bed of nails compared with Birmingham. A university faculty of divinity is likely to think it knows more about theology than any bishop can.
Edwin Chapman, Reading, Berks.

QUESTION: Why can't you keep bananas in the fridge?

☐ THE answer to this, and to most questions pertaining to the science of food, can be found in Harold McGee's *On Food and Cooking*. Bananas grow in hot climates, so they are unused to the cold. If they're kept at a cold temperature, the enzymes that enable them to ripen are inhibited. And as those enzymes become inactive, other enzymes operate more efficiently. Some cause cell damage, while others (browning enzymes) cause the skin to blacken. Bananas, avocados, citrus fruits, pineapples, tomatoes and melons all do best if stored at around 10°C.
Richard Ehrlich, London NW5.

☐ THE answer from Richard Ehrlich, far from dissuading me from keeping bananas in the fridge, only confirms my habit. Fortunately for the suppliers, banana-eaters are divided into two fairly equal camps: those who like the delicate flavour of the green (unripe?) banana and those who prefer the quite different strong flavour of the yellow (over?)ripe banana. Using cold to inhibit the enzymes which aid the ripening process is just what is needed by the 'greens' but should be avoided by the other camp. As for the blackening of the skin, personally I never eat it.
Maurice J. Richardson, Hatfield, Herts.

☐ TRAVELLING on a banana boat plying between Liverpool and the Cameroons, one learns a lot about bananas. They mustn't be bruised, so the ship takes a zig-zag course to avoid rough seas; they mustn't get too warm or they will ripen too soon; and especially they must not be allowed to get too cold (below 52°F the enzymes that bring about the ripening process are killed and the bananas stay green for ever). Actually, once nicely ripened, they can safely be kept in a fridge.
(Dr) P. M. Edwards, Bath.

QUESTION: What causes travel sickness? Are there any cures other than pills and what is the best type of car to buy to avoid this?

☐ IN MOST cases the cause is the driver, not the car. Drivers who swoop round corners, brake from 60 mph to zero in 50 yards or take off from 0 to 60 in 10 seconds flat are the culprits.
R. Legg, Helston, Cornwall.

☐ THE brain accepts information about our position and movement from our eyes, our organs of balance in our ears and from position and pressure sensors throughout our body. Travel sickness is usually caused by not providing an appropriate visual input (it can be caused by reading in the back of a car, for example). A simple solution is to look outside, preferably forwards. In general, a car with a rough or harsh ride will cause less sickness than one with a soft, spongy suspension.
(Dr) Guy Lightfoot, West Kirby, Wirral.

☐ BEFORE driving to Italy in our wallowing Citroën I made my long-suffering 11-year-old daughter sit on a copy of the *Guardian* − as advised by our local basket-maker. After twisting and turning our way up the scenic route of the Grand St Bernard Pass in the Alps and down again, feeling very green myself, I inquired how she felt. 'I think I'm hungry,' she said. After another tortuous drive that never fails to make us all ill, she answered: 'I'm fine, why?' I wonder if this works for anyone else, and why?
Christine Hare, Rooks Bridge, Somerset.

☐ HOME-MADE ginger biscuits are a very effective remedy. Make them with double the normal amount of powdered ginger and remember to save some for the return journey.
Peggy Loy, Maidstone, Kent.

☐ I AM surprised no one has so far recommended Sea Bands. These are elasticated wrist bands worn by the sufferer during journeys. They are said to work on acupuncture principles by exerting pressure, via a plastic stud, on a particular point near the wrist. My husband's is a typical success story. He had previously tried many different pills, with little effect. Wearing Sea Bands he was able to enjoy a sea trip from Ullapool in a near gale, with a stomach full of fish and chips. The bands are available from most large chemists.
Judy Jackson, Little Hayfield.

☐ NONE of the answers is wholly satisfactory. Motion sickness occurs because the brain receives conflicting information from the various organs of sense. Particularly important are the semi-circular canal balance organs in the middle ear which tell if you are standing or lying even with closed eyes. If the eyes say you are upright, and the canals say you are leaning, then loss of lunch may follow. The way to avoid travel sickness in a car is to 'bank' into the bends as the car turns. The driver does this naturally as the steering wheel is turned and held, thus they lean to the right as they steer to the right. However, a passenger, unless they take active action, will tend to be thrown to the left during a right-hand bend. Leaning the head to the same direction as the bend means that the centrifugal force of the turn is allowed for, and the semi-circular canals only feel a downward pull, albeit slightly stronger than normal gravity. If the head is allowed to be thrown outwards, then the canals feel a lateral force akin to lying when the eyes inform that they are vertical. Nausea will follow, and is commoner with a driver who goes faster round bends, generating stronger centrifugal forces. Whether or not there are beneficial effects to the eating of ginger biscuits I do not know, but as to copies of the *Guardian* under the posteriors of sufferers, there is more logic than may appear to this, though any newspaper

will do. The point is that several sheets of paper are slightly slippery. To sit comfortably on a slippery surface in a moving vehicle requires some movement to avoid being thrown about. The natural tendency as your bottom slides to the left is to lean to the right, and thus produce the banking of the head so essential to avoid travel sickness. The other offerings for travel sickness, such as big cars or earthing devices, have little effect *per se*. However, belief plays a part, and perhaps faith in a concept can overcome a little centrifugal force. After all, if faith can move mountains, keeping lunch down should be a doddle.
(Dr) Stephen Seddon.

QUESTION: Does any country other than Britain have an unwritten constitution?

☐ ONLY the United Kingdom and Israel lack a single document (or group of documents) containing all the most important rules about the system of government. New Zealand was in the same position until 1986, when it adopted a Constitution Act.
Rodney Brazier, Reader in Constitutional Law, University of Manchester.

QUESTION: Was there really room for '15 men on a dead man's chest' in R. L. Stevenson's book *Treasure Island*? Would they have been sitting or standing? And were they sober?

☐ YES, there would have been room for 15 men. The reference is to a small island called Dead Chest, south of Tortola in the British Virgin Islands, where the notorious pirate Blackbeard (alias Edward Teach) was supposed to have abandoned men who disobeyed his orders. With little or no fresh water, a bottle of rum is probably all these unfortunate men had to quench their thirst under the tropical sun before they expired.

Lorimer Poultney, Norwich.

☐ IT IS not 'a dead man's chest' but 'the dead man's chest', i.e. Captain Flint's coffin (pirate humour). Flint originally set sail with a crew of 75, buried the treasure but died before he could get back to England, being survived by only 15 of the crew – 'Drink and the devil had done for the rest', as the lyric continues. But of those 15 only one, Billy Bones, managed to return, as becomes clear in the final chapter of *Treasure Island* when Jim Hawkins quotes the lines 'With one man of her crew alive / What put to sea with seventy-five' (pirate grammar). It is a common mistake to think that the 'chest' is a treasure chest but it is clear from Chapter 32 of the book that the enormous hoard was buried in 'several packing cases', which had been looted by Ben Gunn, who hid the treasure in the cave where it was eventually located.

Ralph Lloyd-Jones, London SE22.

☐ THE two previous correspondents omit some significant details. Blackbeard once marooned 15 of his crew on Dead Man's Chest (a small barren island in the Virgin Islands) with one sword and one bottle of rum to test their meanness, and picked up the survivors after a few days. A relative of R. L. Stevenson (his uncle, I think) had visited the Virgin Islands and the stories he told inspired *Treasure Island*. Norman Island was the basis for Treasure Island itself. There are several outcrops of limestone in the Virgin Islands which have been eroded by the sea into piles of boulders. Dead Man's Chest is one, and has the squat, flat profile of a rib cage. Fallen Jerusalem is another such island. An outcrop on the shore of Virgin Gorda (literally 'fat virgin') forms The Baths. Incidentally, the Queen is said to get her table salt from Salt Island where the unusual profile of the south shore

and the infrequency of tides combine to make a natural salt pan.
(Mrs) Kathryn Shrimpey, London W2.

QUESTION: I have been told that it is illegal to drive a car in bare feet. Is this true?

☐ IT IS not an offence to drive in bare feet provided that you are able to operate the controls safely. This would preclude drivers with wet or sweaty feet. Whether fellow passengers would find barefoot driving offensive is another issue.
John Hutson, RAC Motoring Services, London NW2.

QUESTION: In Victorian stories, people who fell in ponds or got wet feet came home sneezing and were put to bed. Is there medical evidence that a healthy person is at risk of 'catching' cold from such experiences?

☐ IN VICTORIAN times and beyond, the 'putting to bed' was prophylactic. Without modern drugs, pneumonia was almost certainly fatal up to the age of five and above the age of 25 – and even between these two ages 50 per cent died. Our Victorian ancestors did not dare take chances.
Allan Wilson, Comrie, Perthshire.

☐ I AM a Welsh Baptist and we practise immersion baptism of adults, sometimes outdoors in winter, or at least in cold weather. It is commonly stated that no one ever caught a cold after being baptised and we like to think this has something to do with the sanctity of the act.
B. Hughes, Roath, Cardiff.

QUESTION: The flight of the boomerang involves fairly complex aerodynamic theory. How did aborigines

**arrive at the correct shape when it took Western races
so much longer even to imagine an aerofoil section?**

☐ IT IS just possible that aboriginal bushmen were inspired
by the naturally cranked shape of a single bird wing to find
or to fashion a crude replica in wood to throw into a rising
bird flock. But it is more likely that the hurling of assorted
pieces of branchwood eventually resulted in the recognition
that forked or bent pieces flew better than straight ones,
especially if they were launched laterally. The natural trajectory of a vertically thrown weapon is a parabola but the
first laterally launched piece of cranked wood that displayed
the inverse effect by climbing as its spinning and irregular
curved surfaces imparted even an incidental degree of aerodynamic lift would have been closely scrutinised by its
thrower for this strange tendency to rise when spears would
be falling. Fascination with the prolonged flight effects of a
spinning 'wing' shape would have led to widespread aware-
ness of the phenomenon within a few generations (if not
years) and, thereafter, thousands of years of trial-and-error
throws with experimental variations on the basic shape
would have resulted in the polished aerodynamic performance of these highly prized flying weapons which, after
billions of closely observed throws, would be as near perfect
as practice can make.
Fred Suett, Liverpool.

☐ FRED Suett's account is reasonable enough, but the question itself is mis-phrased. An aboriginal boomerang-maker
intending to make a normal hunting weapon (the most
common type) selects an angled branch of dense wood, such
as mulga, with a slight twist to the grain. This facilitates the
rubbing-down of the piece to form a relatively flat undersur-
face with an increase of incidence (a slight tip-up of the
leading edge) towards the tips. This is the main reason for
sustained flight, as experiments this century with model

aircraft wings show that for chords less than four inches (distance across the wing) the aerofoil effect rapidly wanes; and boomerang blades are usually less than three inches. The reason for the apparent aerofoil section is partly to reduce air resistance and partly to provide a fairly sharp forward edge to stun or break leg bones of the quarry (small wallaby, bandicoot, etc.). So the 'aerofoil' section, being thickest in the middle, was almost certainly never intended as such, as true aerofoils are thickest about one-third or less from the leading edge, and must be regular and smooth. The boomerang's stable flight is due largely to gyroscopic effect, and the main hunting type of boomerang, heavy and with only a slight curve or angle, is often not intended to return to the thrower.

Len Clarke A.R.Ae.S., Uxbridge.

QUESTION: Why do clocks with Roman numerals represent four as IIII and not as IV?

☐ SOME 50 years ago I was an instrument maker at RAF Halton, where the subject was much discussed. One exotic theory is that I and V were the initial letters of the Roman god, Jupiter (IVPITER), at a period when the letters J and U were not employed. IIII was used instead of IV to avoid offending the deity. It has also been suggested that counting the number of Is, Vs and Xs on the dial of a IIII-type clock gives four Xs, four Vs and 20 Is, which amounts to four identical XVIIIIs – which might have been easier and more economical to cast. Examining old clock faces, however, shows that the groups were normally cast in one block and not assembled from separate digits. A more plausible theory is that visually the IIII balances the VIII better than IV and it could even be that the Romans did not actually use IV. Certainly IIII has been in use since the sixteenth century at least.

Peter Prictoe, Barnsley, S. Yorks.

QUESTION: Do scarecrows really work?

□ No, but because none of them registers for benefit they do not count as unemployed either.
E. Crundwell, Emsworth, Hants.

QUESTION: Is there any evidence that heading a football over a period of years can result in brain damage?

□ ACCORDING to the *Guinness Book of Soccer*, Rodney Marsh, the Queens Park Rangers forward in the 1969–70 season, was given a permanent disability pension of 27 shillings as the result of deafness in one ear caused by heading the ball.
Frank Arthurs, Bath.

□ THE *Guinness Book* is wrong. Rodney Marsh lost the hearing in one ear and qualified for a pension because he collided with a goalpost in the act of scoring the winning goal for Fulham (not QPR) at Leicester on 21 September 1963. He was then only 18 years old, and in his fourth League game. Ever the extrovert, he headed the post as well as the ball. The former, being harder than his head, did the damage that the latter could never do.
David Prole, Woodham, Surrey.

□ THIS was discussed in a paper given to the Manchester Association of Engineers in March 1972 by Prof. W. Johnson, entitled 'The impact, rebound and flight of a well-inflated pellicle as exemplified in Association Football'. Many effects of a moving football were described and in the following discussion the mechanics of boxing knockouts and heading footballs were debated. It was noted that professional footballers instinctively make no attempt to head a ball travelling at over 40 mph – obviously for their own protection, to keep the impact damage to the brain to an 'acceptable' level.

H. J. V. Charlton, Hon. Keeper of Archives, Manchester Association of Engineers, Sale, Cheshire.

QUESTION: Who was the Frenchman who proposed the theory that the wind is caused by trees waving their branches? Did he have any other interesting theories?

□ THE questioner may be referring to the work of the Swiss (not French) genetic epistemologist Jean Piaget. His investigations into the development of reasoning in children included what he described as 'transductive reasoning' in which the child assumes a causal relationship between events which occur together. Piaget reports a child who said one afternoon: 'It isn't afternoon because I haven't had my nap.' The specific example of the tree 'causing' wind may derive from Chudovsky's book *From Two to Five* (published in 1963) which reports a child as saying: 'Daddy please cut down this pine tree – it makes the wind. After you cut it down the weather will be nice and mother will let me go for a walk.' Incidentally, reasoning from correlation to cause is not confined to children's logic – as the pronouncements of almost any politician will confirm.

(Dr) Dennis Bancroft, School of Education, The Open University, Milton Keynes.

□ ON Tortola in the British Virgin Islands during Hurricane David some years back, trees were waving their branches so hard that they were falling over. The Cable and Wireless communications centre had an emergency generator which started automatically when mains power failed, ensuring there was no break in essential communications. After this happened several times, I was visited by a neighbour who asked us to have the generator attended to because 'every

time it started up the whole neighbourhood had a power cut'.
Peter Kemp, Long Melford, Suffolk.

QUESTION: I get a hangover from red wine but none from white. Why?

☐ HANGOVERS are usually caused by dehydration following excess alcohol. Sometimes a hangover results after just two or three glasses of red wine or port. This is because these drinks naturally contain substances that can trigger a headache or migraine in sensitive people. The polyphenols including tannin, which are found in the skins of red grapes, are the compounds incriminated. White wine contains fewer polyphenols and tannin, and is less likely to give you a headache, unless of course you drink too much. Here is a list of some alcoholic drinks in decreasing order of likelihood of giving you a migraine: port, red wine, brandy, dark ale, lager, white wine and white spirits (vodka, gin, white rum).
(Dr) Tom Sanders, Reader in Nutrition, Dept of Nutrition and Dietetics, King's College, London W8.

QUESTION: How can I buy a Trabant car?

☐ NEW Trabants are not available in Britain but, if you are keen enough, the expense involved in going to a former Eastern bloc country and personally importing one is lower than the price of a new Mini. I bought my six-month-old four-stroke Trabant in Budapest for £1,200 and drove it back without any trouble, only to face a 37.5 per cent levy at Dover (10 per cent car tax, 10 per cent import tax, plus VAT). Add to that third-party fire and theft insurance – £300 a year in my case – and the car was on the road in Britain, complete with H-plates, for just over £2,000.

Exporting the car from Hungary was an administrative nightmare, despite extensive help from Hungarian friends in the face of amused officials. Like all new cars, it must face an MOT after three years and I am not allowed to sell it because Trabants have not been crash-tested for 'type approval' in Britain and can only be imported for personal use. The four-stroke Trabant was made in East Germany shortly before the factory was closed earlier this year. It was made solely for the Polish and Hungarian markets. It looks like the infamous, smelly two-stroke but has a made-under-licence VW Polo engine and does more than 30 miles to the gallon. Many of the parts it contains are also to be found in Skodas, Wartburgs and Polos, and should be available here. The car also comes with a four-volume handbook (available in English) and an enormous East European-style tool set. If you want a two-stroke Trabi, go to Germany, where they are practically being given away. But be prepared to face the wrath of your eco-friendly friends.

A. Duval Smith, registration number: H805 YYW.

QUESTION: Do dogs bark with regional accents?

☐ ONLY in Berkshire.
Ken Stark, Leeds, Yorks.

☐ I DON'T know about dogs barking with accents, but they certainly react to what they deem to be an 'unacceptable' human one. My three test proofs, decades ago, that my English (the language of my adopted country) was beginning to sound 'normal' were, in this order: being able to converse on the phone without having to repeat everything; young children responding as they would to any native; and dogs no longer snarling at me when I spoke to them.
G. Hanko, Ealing, London W13.

☐ ONLY another dog could tell, because perception of accent

depends on potential ability to speak the language. A human can't 'speak' like an animal, so there is no way of recognising the accent of a dog any more than that of a horse or a blackbird.
Laurie Smith, Carshalton, Surrey.

QUESTION: Why do men have fewer ribs than women?

☐ MEN and women have 12 pairs of ribs (a few individuals have 13 or 11 pairs). The idea that men have fewer ribs than women is widespread but wrong, perhaps deriving from the biblical story of Eve being made from one of Adam's ribs.
Steve Harper, Lecturer in Anatomy and Physiology, Thanet Technical College, Broadstairs, Kent.

☐ IT'S untrue. There is, however, a disease known as cervical rib which produces a single extra rib at the base of the neck. This is very rare indeed and can occur in either sex.
James Mercer, Sheffield.

QUESTION: Is it true that King Juan Carlos of Spain is also king of Jerusalem? If so, how did the title come about, and what powers does it confer?

☐ WHILE it is true that there is still a titular king of Jerusalem, the title is held by Otto von Habsburg, not the present king of Spain. It originates from the conquest of the Holy Land by the First Crusade in 1099. Godfroi de Bouillon became ruler of Jerusalem, then his brother, Baudouin, became king proper, on Godfroi's death, in 1100. As with many regal titles, the kingship survived the loss of the land to which it pertained (Queen Elizabeth II is still Duke of Normandy). The 'kingship' of Jerusalem passed through French noble families and was held by the House of Lorraine. The title passed into the Habsburg dynasty when

François de Lorraine married Maria Theresa of Austria, and
so also became Holy Roman Emperor. The Austrian Habs-
burgs are very much alive today, even if denuded of empire.
Otto von Habsburg is now an MEP and dreams of a pan-
European federal-democratic version of the Holy Roman
Empire (*Guardian*, 30 May 1991). And who can say we are
not heading in that direction?
Ian Murland, Warrington, Cheshire.

**QUESTION: Why was St Paul's Cathedral unscathed in
the Second World War? Did the Germans have a policy
of not attacking national monuments?**

☐ ST PAUL'S was as vulnerable as the rest of London. For
example, on the night of 29 December 1940, the City
was subjected to an intense attack by the Luftwaffe. Thousands of incendiary bombs were dropped and large areas
around St Paul's were set ablaze. The St Paul's Watch had
installed tanks, baths and pails of water at vulnerable
points about the roof. Small squads with stirrup-pumps
fought each fire separately. Two days later, the Government
appealed for the formation of voluntary street fire parties
to protect buildings, and by January a statutory order
was made requiring fire-watching parties in business and
industrial premises. The aim was to reduce calls to the fire
brigade.
Marianne Saabye, London Fire and Civil Defence Authority.

☐ THE Germans did have a policy for attacking national
monuments for a time in what were termed the Baedeker
raids by the Luftwaffe during April, May and June 1942.
But these were in response to the RAF bombing of Lübeck
in late March. Described by the Chiefs of Staff as a progressive destruction and dislocation of the enemy's economic
system to undermine morale, Lübeck was not seen as a
military target. An enraged Hitler then ordered attacks

on cities known specifically for their architectural attractions. The aim was to hit every building marked with three stars in the Baedeker guidebooks. Targets included Exeter, Bath, Norwich, Canterbury and York. However, that St Paul's remained unscathed during the Blitz of 1940 was possibly a more technical matter. Its dome, in daytime, or when reflecting moonlight, was a convenient navigational aid.
Dennis Hicks, Gravesend, Kent.

☐ ALL those with a religious faith, like myself, liked to believe it was divine intervention that left St Paul's standing. However, I remember very clearly intense anger among those who travelled to the City every day; they said that all the fire-fighting services were concentrated on the Cathedral, and hundreds of office buildings and warehouses were left to burn. The Germans certainly did not have a policy of not attacking national monuments – witness Coventry Cathedral, etc. The bombing in 1940–41 of London was mainly to destroy civilian morale. I'm sure the Government thought that saving St Paul's was a boost to civilian morale, and so it was proved to be, in the main.
Mrs Dorothy Spriggs, Sunbury-on-Thames, Middx.

QUESTION: As an atheist, I would rather not be buried on consecrated ground. Is there any law to stop me being buried in my garden or in a favourite piece of downland?

☐ SURELY an atheist would regard consecrated ground as no different from any other ground.
Robert Keys, Sturminster Newton, Dorset.

☐ TO AVOID being buried on consecrated ground, one need only ensure that there is a secular funeral. Any subsequent burial will certainly be in a local authority cemetery, which will not be consecrated. Only churchyards are consecrated and even then many extensions to churchyards are unconsecrated (mainly because of legal complications). It is perfectly possible to be buried in your own garden, as long as you have the permission of the local authority environmental health officer. There may be problems, as registered cemeteries have to be at least 100 yards from the walls of the nearest dwelling. However, Tony Walter records in his book *Funerals and How to Improve Them* (Hodder & Stoughton, 1990) that the owner of a medieval manor house got permission to be interred in the house's chapel, so all things are possible. Also bear in mind that after death your body is the property of your next of kin; and, no matter what your wishes, it is they who have the right of disposal.

(Rev. Dr) Mike Parsons, St Augustine's Vicarage, Derby.

QUESTION: Why is it that we never hear of people developing cancer of the heart?

☐ LARGELY because primary tumours of the heart are very rare. A benign tumour, the myxoma, is the most common type to be seen. Estimates of frequency of primary tumours is in the order of one in 10,000. On the other hand, secondary spread of tumours arising elsewhere and settling in the lining of the heart, the pericardium, although not necessarily causing symptoms, is much more common, being found at post mortem in around 5 per cent of people with cancers starting elsewhere.

(Dr) A. L. Clark, National Heart and Lung Institute, London SW3.

☐ IN THE Cancer Ward of Solzhenitsyn's novel, the notes of one patient contain the sentence of death: 'Tumor cordis; casus inoperabilis'.

Anthony Ferner, Leamington Spa, Warwicks.

QUESTION: 'Bob's your uncle.' Who is Bob?

☐ ROBERT Arthur Talbot Gascoyne-Cecil, third Marquess of Salisbury and Prime Minister in 1887, when he promoted (not for the first time) his nephew A. J. Balfour to be Chief Secretary for Ireland in a move widely interpreted as an unusually literal act of nepotism. Balfour himself later became Prime Minister, and later still the Foreign Secretary who made the Balfour Declaration in 1917. Originally 'Bob's your uncle' was presumably an ironic or jocular catchphrase meaning 'It's all right for you' (i.e. you've got an Uncle Bob), though now it has lost its tone.
B. A. Phythian, Keston, Kent.

QUESTION: Is there a limit to the number of tunes that can be composed?

☐ IF THERE isn't, can someone please tell Andrew Lloyd Webber.
Peter Barnes, Milton Keynes.

☐ PROBABLY there is, but the number is very large. Take a four-bar melody in simple 4/4 time, i.e. 16 notes, and using just one octave, then the number of different tunes is eight to the power of 16, which is 280 million. Many of these tunes will be boringly useless. If they were played at the rate of one every 10 seconds day and night, it would take 88 years to play them all. So while there is a limit, for practical purposes the number is limitless.
David Land, Edinburgh.

☐ IT LOOKS for a moment as though there might be, since pitch, in the equal-temperament system, is limited to trans-positions of the same 12 pitches. But the number of potential

tunes could not be arrived at by counting the permutations of the 12 pitches. Other factors, such as rhythmic combinations, repetitions of notes within a tune and even octave transpositions of individual notes could only be arbitrarily limited. And, given two tunes, identical in pitch but different in tempo and rhythm, and with different repetitions of notes, no one would say they were the same tune. Of course, the number of good tunes is probably not infinite, but since no one could ever agree on what constitutes a good tune, or on what factors distinguish a good tune from a bad one, it would be impossible to say what that number could be.
Philip Hensher, London SW6.

QUESTION: Which is the safest seat on a London tube train?

☐ WHEN one is faced by loonies, Moonies, drunks, 'in car' buskers, a tramp whose odour is as high as his luck is low necessitating the evacuation of the entire car, the occasional belligerent begger and the inhalation by force of proximity of fellow passengers' (sorry – customers') breath, laden with colds, flu and garlic, one can only assume the safest seat on a London tube train to be the one safely locked away at the front, occupied by the driver.
Ian D. Harragan, London N1.

QUESTION: Why, when a footballer scores three goals in a game, is it called a 'hat-trick'?

☐ THE term originated in cricket and refers to the bowler's taking of three wickets in successive balls. George Macdonald Frazer (*Flashman's Lady*, set in 1843) claims the first use for Flashman. When he takes his third wicket (by cheating), the victim, Alfred Mynn, presents Flashman with his straw boater as he leaves the field with the words: 'That

trick's worth a new hat any day, youngster.' More seriously, Eric Partridge (*Historical Slang*), giving 1882 as the probable date of origin, says it entitled its professional performer to a collection, or to a new hat from his club. Amateur players, being gentlemen, could, presumably, afford their own hats.
Ramin Minova, Moseley, Birmingham.

☐ DAVID Harris, the great Hambledon bowler of the 1780s, was presented with a gold-laced hat after a fine spell of bowling, though not actually taking three wickets with successive deliveries. Around 1800 the first top hat, a white beaver, came into vogue and was awarded by some clubs to bowlers who took three wickets with successive deliveries. This practice grew until the late 1800s when the tasselled cap, boater and pill-box cap made the top hat no longer *de rigueur*. The hat-trick was then coined by other sports to indicate a three-fold success.
Steve Pittard, Langport, Somerset.

☐ WHEN football was in its infancy, and hence footballers were not professional, top scorers were not rewarded for their goals. If a player scored three goals in a match, a hat, or similar container, would be passed round for donations. I presume that only the home supporters would actually chip in.
Peter Orme, Winchester, Hants.

QUESTION: Can a plant die of old age?

☐ PLANTS certainly have life cycles, just as mammals. They say an oak tree grows for 300 years, rests for 300 years and then spends 300 years gracefully expiring. Sadly, an old tree is frequently considered dangerous (it will drop the occasional branch) and unsightly (it goes bald, or stagheaded – quite becoming in an old codger). Old trees are rare old characters that need to be watched over. The rough guide to

age is: one inch of circumference (measured four feet up the trunk) equals one year of growth.
S. Rodway, London W14.

☐ THE lifecycle of a plant may be divided into germination, seedling establishment, growth and development, flowering and fruiting, senescence and death. Senescence is the sequence of events allowing the deterioration of cells and organs, which will lead to the death of all or part of a plant. This is largely dependent on plant species. Most evergreens keep their leaves for a couple of years before they die and are shed; bristle cone pine has functional needles for up to 30 years. The leaves on deciduous trees and shrubs die each year, but the stem and root systems stay alive for several years. In perennial grasses and herbs the above-ground system dies every year but the crown and roots remain viable. In herbaceous annuals leaf senescence progresses from old to young leaves, followed by death of stem and roots after the plant has flowered, leaving only the seed to survive.
Lucy H. Smith, Harpenden, Herts.

QUESTION: The week of seven days is part of the Judaeo-Christian tradition. Pre-Christian pagan traditions did not use it, so why are the days of the week in almost all European languages named after pagan gods?

☐ IT IS incorrect to say that pre-Christian traditions 'did not use it'. Inscriptions from Pompeii – which must date before the town's destruction by Vesuvius in AD 79 – record the days of the week in their modern order and refer specifically to 'dies solis' (i.e. Sunday) and to 'dies Jovis' (i.e. jeudi, that is, Thursday). In other words, the seven-day week, with days named after pagan gods in the current fashion, was already in use in pagan Rome in the first century AD. Thus it is in no way surprising that in AD 321 the Emperor

Constantine decreed that the 'dies solis' (Sunday) should be the day of rest for Christians, to separate them from the Jews, and indeed to set himself up against Jehovah.

J. C. Mann, Emeritus Professor of Roman-British History and Archaeology, University of Durham.

☐ ALTHOUGH the seven-day week was not adopted in Europe for official use until the Christian period, its origins are much more ancient, since they lie in the astronomy/astrology of the Babylonians. It was they who identified the seven known planets with their seven greatest deities – for example calling the beautiful morning and evening star after Ishtar, the Goddess of Love – and allotted each a day to rule. In Hellenistic times the Greeks, with their adoption of Babylonian astrology, dropped their own ancient names for the planets and also began to call them after the gods, translating the Babylonian names with their nearest Greek equivalents. Ishtar's planet was now 'the Star of Aphrodite'. When further translated into Latin, these became the planetary names with which we are now familiar – Sol, Luna, Mars, Mercury, Jupiter, Venus and Saturn (and the connections are still clear in French and other Romance languages). However, the Anglo-Saxons translated the planetary names yet again, using the names of their own deities, so that in English we now have days of Tiw, Woden, Thor and Freya (they seem to have given up on Saturn). The system spread east as well as west. In India, the Greek god names were translated into their Sanskrit equivalents, giving Ravivara, the day of the Sun, Somavara, the day of the Moon, and so on. These names are still current throughout India and south-east Asia.

Valerie Roebuck, MA PhD, Manchester 16.

☐ SLAVONIC languages such as Polish and Russian have secular name-days (for example Thursday is 'fourth day' and Friday is 'fifth day'). Hungarian borrows Friday from Slavonic languages and has different but equally secular

names for the other days; for example, Sunday is called 'market day'.
Kola Krauze, London W2.

QUESTION: Why is it that the keys on push-button telephones are numbered from the top downwards, but vice versa on computers?

☐ RESEARCH as far back as 1955 showed that the 1-2-3 arrangement conforms to people's expectations better than the 7-8-9 arrangement, but the same research also showed that people did not expect there to be any performance difference between the two layouts. In 1963, the 7-8-9 arrangement was adopted as the British Standard (BS 1909) and the first research on performance with the two arrangements was conducted in Cambridge. Unfortunately the research demonstrated that the 1-2-3 layout led to significantly better performance than 7-8-9. This research has been replicated on a number of occasions. Companies designing numeric keypads therefore had two conflicting pieces of information and I do not know how their decisions were made. However, whatever the issues were then, the problem now is that neither industry can easily change without upsetting many experienced users. The same problem occurs for alphanumeric keypads, where we now know that QWERTY is not the best arrangement, but the major difficulties of changing to better keyboards (e.g. the Dvorak keyboard) are deemed to outweigh the benefits.
David Gilmore, Psychology Dept, University of Nottingham.

QUESTION: We are told that our hearts operate by electricity. Where is this electricity generated and to what power?

☐ THE source of electricity is the ability of individual cells to concentrate potassium ions within them and to expel sodium from their interior. They can do this because, like most other cells, they have a biochemical ion pump in their outer cell membrane which uses metabolic energy generated within the cells using either oxygen or glucose. Because of the action of this pump the cell interior is rich in potassium and poor in sodium ions, in contrast to the fluid surrounding it which is rich in sodium and poor in potassium ions. Small voltages are generated across the cell membrane as these ions, which carry a positive charge, have a tendency to flow down their concentration gradient across the cell membrane. In a resting cell, the membrane is more permeable to potassium than to sodium ions, and the interior of the cell is at a negative voltage relative to the outside (this is termed 'polarised'). The voltage is less than 0.1 of a volt. At the start of a heart beat, the pacemaker sends out an electrical signal that triggers in neighbouring cells an increase in the permeability of the membrane to sodium ions. This causes the voltage across the membrane to reverse so that the cell interior is now at a positive voltage relative to the outside. This process, depolarisation, in turn triggers a depolarisation in neighbouring cells and the effect is a wave of depolarisation spreading across the heart. In each cell the depolarisation allows calcium ions to enter the cell, and this triggers the cell's contraction. The energy used by the ion pump to set up voltages across the cell membranes in the heart is very small. A resting heart works at about 5 watts but only about 1 per cent of this will be used to pump ions. Even this small fraction cannot be put to external use because the electrical energy of ions flowing in and out of cells is not directly available.

Ron Jacob, Physiology Group, King's College, London W8.

QUESTION: Why is the most common form of heterosexual coupling called the missionary position?

☐ I MAY be wrong, but isn't the missionary position the one recommended by lay preachers?
Philip Oliver, Burton upon Trent, Staffs.

☐ THIS appears to be so-called not because it was used by missionaries (although that was probably the case) but because it was the position missionaries are supposed to have advocated for the 'lesser races' they were preaching to. There seem to be two reasons for this preference. The face-to-face position was thought more 'civilised' than other 'animalistic' ones and, secondly, it literally put the man on top. In this way the position embodied two key aspects of the nineteenth-century middle-class view of the world. The evidence of sex positions in the past suggests that it was by no means the most preferred and perhaps not the most common. Presumably the missionaries encountered a situation where it was not so common otherwise they would not have had to advocate it. The rise of the missionary position, therefore, seems to be related to the intensification of a male-dominated, imperialist, class society. But contemporary sex surveys also suggest that both men and women often get more pleasure from alternative positions. Readers sympathetic towards the Labour Party's current abandonment of class politics might like to consider the significance this has for their own lives. Not only are revolutionary positions more politically correct, they are also likely to be more fun.
Mike Haynes, Telford Socialist Workers Party, Salop.

☐ I AM fairly certain that Mike Haynes of the Socialist Workers Party has, unsurprisingly, adopted the wrong position over missionaries. The 'missionary position' was not advocated by them but was their conventional mode and observed as such by Trobriand Islanders in the depth of the Polynesian night – and eventually reported to Malinowski et al. (qv). One matter is, however, illuminated by Haynes: the reluctance of SWP members to look one another in the eye.
R. A. Leeson, Broxbourne, Herts.

QUESTION: Why do your fingers go wrinkly in the bath?

☐ I ONCE asked champion swimmer Adrian Moorhouse whether he went wrinkly at the edges after hours of cranking up those practice lengths. The look of surprise on his face revealed that he had never even thought of the possibility. This suggests that whatever happens to people in their baths depends on some combination of hot water and soap.
Humphrey Evans, London N7.

☐ THE skin of the fingers is covered by a protective, waterproof layer called keratin. Under normal conditions this is translucent and flattened. However, when placed in water for some time, the protein begins to absorb water, becoming swollen and opaque. The top layer of the skin (epidermis) is tethered down to the lower layer (dermis) by means of 'papillary ridges', which form the fingerprint. The swollen keratin in the epidermis is therefore held down along the lines of the fingerprint, causing wrinkling.
(Dr) Janet Menage, Rugby, Warwicks.

QUESTION: It might be expected that lungs would be more efficient (as well as sloughing off infection more easily) if they were open-ended with a once-through air flow like gills. Why did gills not evolve for use by land animals?

☐ 'WHY?' is a question that cannot strictly be answered by scientific study, for we cannot observe purpose: the most we can do is to speculate as to the advantages of certain structures and mechanisms that led to their selection in evolution. On that basis, to achieve adequate gas exchanges land animals must expose blood to air over a large surface – about the size of a tennis court in human lungs. In a once-through system this would lead to large losses of water and

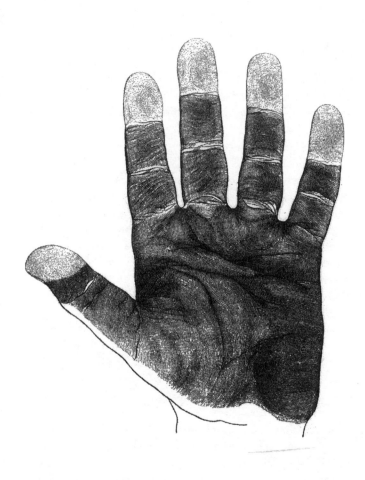

of body heat. In the 'tidal' breathing system we actually have, however, the upper respiratory tract functions as a 'countercurrent exchanger': that is, incoming air is warmed and moistened before it reaches the respiratory surface, and much of the heat and moisture are recovered before the air is exhaled. By this means the losses are reduced to levels the animal can compensate for.

(Prof.) Romaine Hervey, Wells, Somerset.

□ IF HUMANS had a similar system to fish we would have to live in a continuous wind or spend our lives running around or live in water. Two questions are then posed. How could we sleep? Would we be able to talk?

B. G. F. Beadle, Kenilworth, Warwicks.

□ IT IS an interesting problem in evolution; not everything can evolve into something entirely different. The analogy, in the present case, would be between a piston engine (pump action) and a jet engine (once through), with the difference that Frank Whittle could start again from scratch, but our ancestors could not. The amphibians and the lung-fishes represent the appropriate evolutionary stages. The tadpole uses gills and a tail in water, and discards both before landing. The evolution of the lung corresponds to finding a new use for an old organ. The lung evolved from the swim bladder of fishes, an air-filled sac just below the backbone, which helps to keep a fish upright and neutrally buoyant. Because the fish needed to be neutrally buoyant at different depths, it had to diffuse gas in and out of the bladder from the blood-stream fairly rapidly across an elastic membrane and vent it (otherwise it would burst!), but it only needed an entrance at one end, like a balloon. So by the time lung-fishes and amphibians evolved, most of the equipment necessary for air-breathing was already in place. It was then too late to evolve a second exit. Squid use a once-through peristaltic system for propulsion, and it is not very efficient, and we do it for digestion and elimination. The other

problem solved is that the lung surface needs to retain
moisture, and we also diffuse the water vapour across the
lung surface. In a once-through system we would have had
to evolve the biological throat-spray as well.
Alex Milne, Newcastle-upon-Tyne.

**QUESTION: Is there a reliable way to get rid of head
lice without using insecticide shampoos?**

☐ ACCORDING to my copy of *Lice* (British Museum Natural
History Economic Series No. 2a, 4th edition, 1969), there
are two ways. Shaving the head is described as a 'very
thorough remedy, but unnecessarily drastic'. The favoured
alternative is to use a special fine-toothed comb which will
effectively remove all lice and nits (the eggs) 'providing the
combing is carefully and conscientiously done'. Damping or
slightly oiling the hair may aid the passage of the comb,
though the booklet claims there is no truth in the belief that
vinegar loosens dead nits and allows them to be easily
removed.
Peter Barnes, Milton Keynes.

☐ EXHAUSTIVE tests in this family have shown that the Body
Shop's Orange Spice shampoo is remarkably effective at
killing lice and nits. To prevent reinfestation, cultivating a
repellently dirty and greasy head of hair is recommended.
Richard Moore, London SE5.

☐ I'M NOT sure about the bacteria but I speak from five
years' experience of not washing my hair and it certainly
isn't dirty. I rinse it once every week or so with plain water to
remove dust. I understand that shampoo opens the porous
structure of hair, making it easily damaged, especially when
wet. A word of advice, though: it takes eight to 10 weeks for
the self-cleaning process to start working.
Donna Swabey, Hillhead, Glasgow.

QUESTION: Why do carousels in fairgrounds turn clockwise in Britain and anti-clockwise in America and on the Continent?

☐ THE fairground, in terms of mechanically driven rides, dates from the latter quarter of the Victorian era when the inventor, genius and one-time mayor of King's Lynn, Frederick Savage, first applied steam to propel a merry-go-round. Roundabouts featuring horses were traditionally very popular and as one normally mounts and dismounts the real animal from its left side it was natural that the ride should rotate clockwise. Savage perfected and patented a system for giving the wooden horses on his carousels a realistic galloping action and, to avoid infringement of these patents, foreign manufacturers designed their rides to rotate anti-clockwise. Although there were English merry-go-rounds that spun anti-clockwise, the clockwise rotation of English carousels and other spinning riding machines has endured to this day.
Shane Seagrave, Bournemouth.

☐ THE anti-clockwise motion of Continental and American carousels did not result from any need to avoid infringing British patents. Just as the early British roundabouts reflected the practice of mounting a horse from the left (and hence necessitated a clockwise motion), the design of their Continental equivalents reflected previous customs. Continental rides evolved from the French carousel, a device for entertainment begun in the seventeenth century. Based on an equestrian sport which had its origins in twelfth-century Turkey and Arabia, the carousel consisted of a small, hand-powered roundabout alongside which a ring hung from a post or gibbet. The riders would attempt to lance the ring as they rode past. Because it was customary to hold the lance in the right hand, the movement of the ride past the target was anti-clockwise. The original purpose of the carousel was to train young members of the nobility for the tournament of ring-spearing. The name itself is derived from the ancient Spanish word *carosella*, meaning 'little war'. The carousel became the pattern for the nineteenth-century American fairground ride builders mainly because many of them – like the German Gustave Dentzel – were immigrants from Continental Europe. This essential difference in historical background also explains why one should never refer to a British roundabout as a carousel.

Graham Downie, Chairman, The Fairground Association of Great Britain, Studley, Warwicks.

QUESTION: What is the purpose of the little hole in the side of a ballpoint pen?

□ THE hole is to equalise the air pressure inside and outside the pen barrel. When a ballpoint pen is used ink is drawn out of the plastic tube in the pen. In sealed pens this causes a drop in pressure inside the pen due to air being drawn down the ink tube and the flow of the ink is inhibited. If, however, air is allowed to enter the pen barrel, the pressure can be brought to that of the environment, and a good flow of ink maintained, hence the little hole in the side of the pen. The situation can be likened to the pouring of a liquid from a (previously sealed) can, such as of condensed milk. One punched hole will give a 'glug-glug' flow, because as the liquid leaves the can, air must enter via the same hole to fill the space vacated by the liquid. If, however, another hole is punched in the opposite side of the can air may enter on one side, while the liquid is poured out of the other, giving a smooth flow. This does not explain why certain mints have holes in the middle – any suggestions?

Peter Finan, Leeds.

QUESTION: Who was the first person to play a guitar into an amplifier?

☐ THE easy answer is a jazz guitarist by the name of Jack Miller. Miller first used his new Rickenbacker Electro Spanish guitar at Grauman's Chinese Theater in Los Angeles in 1932. He later wrote a series of articles for *Downbeat* magazine in which he described himself as 'the first to play electric guitar'. However, since the invention of the telephone mouthpiece pickup by Alexander Graham Bell (1876), all sorts of methods of electrically amplifying musical instruments had been tried, with little practical success. Throughout the 1920s, many guitarists and DIY enthusiasts tinkered with ways of making the guitar louder, producing prototype electric guitars and basses, and primitive amplifiers based on relatively new valve radio technology, though none ever made it into production. The coil-and-magnet guitar pickup as used today was invented around 1930, and the first electric guitars (made by Rickenbacker and National) went on sale to the public in 1931. If the questioner wants to be strictly accurate, George Beauchamp, the man generally credited with the invention of the guitar pickup, was almost certainly the first to play through an amplifier. One last point: amplification helped transform the guitar from a provider of rhythmic backing into a lead instrument that could compete with the horns of the 1930s jazz and swing bands. Among the first people to play lead guitar through an amp were Charlie Christian and Eddie Durham, the latter apparently being the first jazz guitarist to take a solo on record (around 1933).

Jon Lewin, Assistant Editor, Making Music, *London EC1.*

QUESTION: In the British flag, the crosses of St Andrew and St Patrick are split off-centre to the cross of St George. Who designed it and has anyone any idea why it was done in this way?

□ THE crosses of St George and St Andrew were combined in a flag on 12 April 1606, in order to provide a common ensign for English and Scottish ships. This was done by placing a white-bordered red cross (for England) over the white cross on blue of Scotland – incidentally only one of several designs suggested at the time. When Ireland was united to Britain by the Act of 1800 it was decided to add a red saltire cross (supposed to represent Ireland) to the other two. This was done by 'counterchanging' the red and white saltires, as in the diagram (below) which shows how the red and white change places at the centre of the flag, then overlaying them with the English cross. The white border to the English cross remained and also overlays the two saltires, making them look as if they have been cut off, although not 'off-centre' as the question suggests. Later, distortion crept in when flags began to be made with the white border needed for the Irish cross being taken from the cross itself rather than from the underlying blue field, which means that the Irish cross is thinner than the Scottish one. This is not in accordance with the original picture or the correct interpretation of the description, which were given in an Order in Council dated 15 November 1800 and a Royal Proclamation made on 1 January 1801. No one knows who selected the original design of 1606, but it seems likely that the then Garter King of Arms, Sir Isaac Heard, designed the model approved by the Privy Council in 1800.

William G. Crampton, Director, The Flag Institute, Chester.

Counterchanged saltires

QUESTION: Is a contract entered into by fax as legally binding as a written or verbal one?

☐ YES.
John Hendy QC, Lincoln's Inn, London WC2.

☐ THE monosyllabic affirmative from John Hendy QC is obviously authoritative but doesn't explain what happens if the fax gets lost in transmission. Under the general law of contract, the acceptance of an offer must be communicated to the offerer before a contract comes into existence. However, in the leading case of *Household Fire Insurance Co.* v *Grant* (1879), the courts decided that, in the case of an acceptance sent by post, acceptance takes place (and the contract is completed) when the letter is put in the letter box, even if it is subsequently lost in the post. Clearly faith in the postal system was higher then than it is today. Does the same rule apply to faxes? If my faxed acceptance gets scrambled in transmission, but I have proof of transmission, is this sufficient to seal a contract? Back to the QCs to answer, please.
David Brown, London SW26.

☐ WHILE it may well be true that a contract entered into by fax is legally binding, a fax itself is still not considered a legal document, whereas a telex is. This is because the older technology of telex includes an exchange of personalised 'answerbacks' at the beginning and end of the message, which is considered proof of transmission and receipt of the complete message by the two parties identified by these 'answerbacks'. Faxes do not always carry such identification of both transmitting and receiving fax numbers, and fax transmission slips are not considered proof that the message has been received complete and legible. For this reason documents such as visas will be issued and money transactions enacted on the authority of a telex but not on the authority of a fax.
A. J. Papard, Telecommunications Officer, London SW11.

□ IN RESPONSE to A. J. Papard, the original question posed postulated an offer and uncontested acceptance. He raises now the problem of an acceptance by fax which is scrambled and thereby not communicated to the offeror. He points to the general rule that the acceptance of an offer must be communicated to the offeror to make a binding contract and refers to the longstanding exception that where it is reasonable to accept by post, postage of the acceptance is sufficient to conclude the contract notwithstanding that it is not received. The extension of that exception to faxes seems dubious, though a case on the point does not yet appear to have come before the courts here. It is dubious because the 'posting rule' is only an exception to the general rule; because the former is regarded as a 'rule of convenience'; because it is applied restrictively; and because it seems inappropriate for the nature of modern faxed communications. Faxes have characteristics which are more likely to persuade a court to invoke the general rule: communication is almost immediate; the offeree receives a transmission report as to effective transmission; the offeror who receives a scrambled fax is able to respond forthwith and so inform the offeree, and has proof of the illegibility of the communication. In short, the convenience of commerce would seem to be best served by the application of the general rule. This has been held to be the case in relation to telexes: *Brinkibon Ltd* v *Stahag Stahl GmbH* (1982) 2AC 34. Thus sending a scrambled fax which hence does not communicate acceptance is unlikely to result in a binding contract.
John Hendy QC, Lincoln's Inn, London WC2.

QUESTION: Is it true that the Mall in London is intended to serve as an aircraft runway for the evacuation of the royal family in an emergency?

□ HONI soit qui au Mall ainsi pense.
A. E. Baker, Kettering, Northants.

☐ THE Mall would not be a suitable landing strip because of its length, its lamp posts and the adjoining high buildings. However, Peter Laurie, in his book *Beneath the City Streets* (Allen Lane, 1970, pages 173–4), claimed that the Broad Walk, in Kensington Gardens, could be used for this purpose. Mr Laurie also speculated that there might be a secret exit from Buckingham Palace to the Victoria Line which runs below. It has also been claimed that a tunnel exists running from the palace down the Mall to the Duke of York steps, where it connects with the network of tunnels and underground bunkers that run below Whitehall to protect the government from rioting mobs. I think the most logical emergency scenario would be for the royal family to go to Paddington station and take a train to the eastern portal of Box Tunnel, where a set of bomb-proof doors provides access to the Central Government War HQ, in Westwells Road, Corsham, just outside Chippenham.
James Rusbridger, Bodmin, Cornwall.

☐ SURELY Budgie the helicopter will rescue them.
Peter Barnes, Milton Keynes.

QUESTION: What is art?

☐ THE definitive answer was provided 30 years ago by Marshall McLuhan: 'Art is anything you can get away with.'
John Whiting, London NW11.

☐ TOLSTOY offers the following definition: 'To evoke in oneself a feeling one has once experienced, and having evoked it in oneself, then, by means of movements, lines, colours, sounds or forms expressed in words, so to transmit that feeling that others may experience the same feeling – that is the activity of art. Art is a human activity, consisting in this, that one man consciously, by means of certain external signs, hands on to others feelings he has lived

through, and that other people are infected by these feelings, and also experience them.' (From *What is Art?* by L. Tolstoy, translated by A. Maude.)
George Crossley, Bradford.

☐ THE best definition I have come across is by James Joyce: 'Art is the human disposition of sensible or intelligible matter for an aesthetic end.'
Wolf Suschitzky, London W2.

☐ A WORK of art is a corner of creation seen through a temperament (Emile Zola).
C. Heritage-Tilley, Winchester, Hants.

☐ ART is a stuffed crocodile (Alfred Jarry, 1873–1907, author of *Ubu Roi*).
Titus Alexander, London E17.

☐ ART is 'pattern informed by sensibility' (Sir Herbert Read, *The Meaning of Art*).
Henry Burns Elliot, Colchester.

☐ LIFE is serious but art is fun (source unknown).
Nathan Wood, Birmingham 15.

☐ I LIKE Tolstoy's definition of art as the ability to transmit a feeling one has experienced to others through 'movements, lines, colours', etc. But surely pornography does this very effectively. Did Tolstoy consider pornography to be art?
Frank Miles, Beckenham, Kent.

☐ NONE of the answers offered last week is satisfactory. McLuhan's 'Art is anything you can get away with' might admit undetected shoplifting or terrorism, neither of which would normally be considered art. Tolstoy's definitions suggest that the essential property of art is its ability to communicate the expression of emotion to a perceiver:

though art often embodies this characteristic, the definition doesn't account for emotional communication, which most people would recognise as 'outside art' in, for example, common expressions of anger or sadness. James Joyce's definition highlights the use of materials for aesthetic ends: this is quite convincing in the implication that a work of art must have been intended to be a work of art by the artist. The problem is that many works which are now widely accepted as art (such as cave paintings and ritual masks) were not made for aesthetic or artistic reasons. The hundreds of thought-provoking attempts to define art all hold true for some art but not for all art, and often are equally valid for things which are not generally understood to be art. Those who become exhausted by their attempts to answer the question with a single definition might take up the advice of the American philosopher Nelson Goodman and rephrase the question: 'when is an object a work of art?' The dynamic character of much of the most interesting art was, I think, well expressed by the artist Jeff Nuttall, who wrote in 1980, in an article entitled 'Art, Politics and Everything Else': 'Art is the skill of examining the range of our perceptions by the making of artefacts . . . Often the last place you're likely to find the perceptions being extended is in the compartment marked "art", which may have been frozen into stasis by devices like the Standards of Good Taste, Proven Criteria, the Maintaining of Tradition. In the drawer marked "art" there may well be no art at all.'
David Ainley, Matlock, Derbyshire.

☐ AS ROCK Hudson said in *Magnificent Obsession*: 'Art is just a boy's name.'
Hugh Raffles, London W14.

QUESTION: Who are B & Q? (The staff don't know.)

☐ THE staff aren't supposed to know. B & Q were pioneers of

the 'Don't ask me I only work here' school of customer relations; answering questions held up shelf stacking. I had the misfortune to work for them back in 1971 when the empire consisted of one DIY superstore at the unfashionable end of Southampton's Portswood Road and a small hardware shop in Sholing. The 'B' in B & Q was Richard Block, the 'Q' David Quayle, two businessmen from Chandlers Ford, Hampshire, who – despite inflicting their staff with Radio One at full volume all day and every day – were quite nice chaps. When Kingfisher bought them out Mr Quayle became a director of Woolco and Mr Block took his fish (he was a pisciculturalist) and money into tax exile in Jersey. I recently heard a rumour that Mr Block had returned to Hampshire as a hypnotherapist.
Dave Juson, Freemantle, Southampton.

QUESTION: Why, when, where and by whom was it decreed that there should be 360 degrees of arc in a complete circle?

☐ IT WAS during the reign of Nebuchadnezzar (605–562 BC) in the Chaldean dynasty in Babylon that the circle was divided into 360 degrees. This was because the Chaldeans had calculated by observation and inference that a complete year numbered 360 days.
Gadfan Morris, Redhill, Surrey.

☐ ABOUT 4,000 years ago, the basis of angular measure for the mathematicians of Babylon was the angle at each of the corners of an equilateral triangle. They did not have decimal fractions and thus found it difficult to deal with remainders when doing division. So they agreed to divide the corner of an equilateral triangle into 60 degrees, because 60 could be divided by 2, 3, 4, 5 and 6 without remainder. Each degree was divided into 60 minutes and each minute into 60 seconds. If the angles at the corners of six equilateral

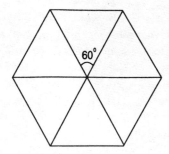

triangles are placed together they form the angle formed by a complete circle (see diagram). It is for this reason that there are six times 60 degrees of arc in the complete circle.
Steve Bolter, Braintree College, Essex.

QUESTION: What is progress?

☐ PROGRESS is when a cannibal uses a knife and fork.
David Still, Market Harborough, Leics., and Martin Lunt, Billinge, nr Wigan, Lancs.

☐ PROGRESS is for 25 years wearing an artificial leg made of metal which needed minimum maintenance (I went 10 years once with no repairs) and was reasonably comfortable – and then having it replaced with a high-tech state-of-the-art leg made of plastic with a complicated knee joint which rattles, knocks, breaks away from rivets, makes very unsocial noises and breaks down approximately every month (two months if you are lucky). I hope this helps to answer the question.
R. A. Butt, Braintree, Essex.

☐ ANY American lawyer will tell you that as pro is to con, so progress is to Congress.
Martin S. Taylor, London SW12.

QUESTION: Is there any way to remove the musty smell from books which have been stored for a long time, without damaging them?

AS once told by an antiquarian book dealer in Belfast e stacked his books like a house of cards and hired students from Queen's University to blow cigar smoke through them. I believed him at the time but I'm not sure I do now.

Muir MacKean, London SW4.

☐ YOU could try the Archives Department of your local council. Years ago, in Nottingham, they treated some books of ours. The books were placed in a fume cupboard for a week, after which they smelt reassuringly clinical.

K. Singh, Cambridge.

☐ WHY try to remove this wonderful smell? It is part of the books' appeal, and it may have unrecognised medical benefits. The father of a friend of mine used to find that breathing in the atmosphere of a well-stocked secondhand bookshop – the mustier the better – was a certain cure for his acute constipation. A bowl of All-Bran just doesn't offer the same satisfaction as a good shelf of old Everyman's Library volumes.

James Carter, Levenshulme, Manchester.

☐ DUST the books gently with a shaving brush or similar and stand them open, in a well-ventilated dry room. As for the smell of musty books having 'unrecognised medical benefits', you should always avoid deliberately putting your nose into an old book and breathing deeply, as germs can be trapped in books and live for years.

Liz Branigan, Bookbinder, Hexham, Northumberland.

☐ JAMES Carter mentions the medical benefits of the smell of secondhand books in treating constipation. I first became aware of this little-known side effect of my interest in old books some years ago, and have been plagued by it ever since. So it is reassuring to know that there are other sufferers. Is there perhaps some medical explanation? If it

hasn't been recognised by the medical establishment yet, it has clearly been acknowledged by the local council at Hay-on-Wye – the 'town of books' – where the public conveniences are modern, clean and, most importantly, large.
Andrew Colley, Basildon, Essex.

QUESTION: There is said to be a Chinese short story consisting of the word 'shi' repeated 72 times. Is there an English translation?

☐ I DON'T know about Chinese, but you can have a conversation in Finnish with words containing only the letters K and O: 'Kokoo koko kokko kokoon!' (Gather the whole fire together!) 'Koko kokkoko?' (The whole fire?) 'Koko kokko.' (The whole fire.)
Marjukka Grover, Clevedon, Avon.

☐ TO TALK about 'shi' as if it were a single word is wrong. In *Mathew's Chinese–English Dictionary* there are 73 different characters, all with the pronunciation 'shi', most with several different meanings per character. When reading Chinese, there is no confusion as each character is distinct in appearance. When speaking Mandarin Chinese, 'shi' can be pronounced in four different tones or pitches: high and flat; rising; falling then rising; falling. In normal conversation, a combination of spoken tone and context enables you to know which 'shi' is being used. It would indeed be possible to write a story using 72 characters pronounced 'shi', but by modern standards it would be stilted and grammatically incorrect. In classical language it would be easier to get away with, but still pushing it a bit. If there is such a story I do not know of it. I did compose a brief example using 24 'shi': 'An official was on his way to the capital when he saw 10 large pigs eating some small red berries. When he rubbed the pigs they were in fact stone corpses. Thus he knew the berries were

poisonous.' An even briefer five 'shi': 'The master is fond of licking lion spittle.'
Tim Askew, Wadham College, Oxford.

QUESTION: Why do we not fall out of bed from time to time when we are asleep?

□ OUR distant ancestors were arboreal apes and presumably slept in trees, as modern chimpanzees and gorillas do (in fact they build nests to sleep in). Apes that fell out of bed would tend to have fewer offspring, so it is likely that our ancestors were the ones that descended from the trees when they were awake. We have inherited their sense of balance.
Andrew West, Surbiton, Surrey.

□ IT HAPPENS to some adults occasionally, and it certainly happens to children. How many parents have not heard the tell-tale bump overhead or in an adjoining room at night?
(Mrs) Valerie R. Stokes, Carlisle, Cumbria.

QUESTION: What are the low and high roads to Scotland, and why should these alternative travel arrangements prevent further lakeside meetings, amorous or otherwise?

□ THE song, 'The Bonnie Banks O' Loch Lomon' ', is usually sung in a jolly marching rhythm. In fact, it is very sad and makes me weep buckets every time I hear it. Scots believe that when they die, wherever they are at the time of death, their souls immediately return to Scotland and reach there via underground passages and caves: this is the 'low road', whereas anyone living who makes the journey is travelling on the ordinary road, the 'high way'. The song is a conversation between two prisoners, one of whom is obviously destined to be executed in the morning, while his companion is to be set free to return home. The soul will travel more

quickly – which is why he will reach Scotland before his companion, but of course, being dead, he will be unable to communicate with his sweetheart.
Isabel Grindley, Cheltenham, Glos.

QUESTION: Why are there no pink cars?

☐ THE main reason for the absence of some colours and shades is the instability of certain pigments. Reds, other than lead oxide base, are notorious faders – for example, the maroons which at one time were the most popular car colours. There was an instance of a pink car in the days when BMC Austin A30s were sold in a coat of pink primer to speed cheap production; customers eager for a new car bought them at finished price, then had to find a local firm to finish spraying to the required colour. A popular story in the motor industry of the 1950s was that the primer tint was classified as Nipple Pink in mock tribute to the 'suckers' who bought these cars.
Wilfrid Burdett, Oxford.

QUESTION: What is the scientific difference between plant life and animal life?

☐ THE fundamental difference is in the way animals and plants take in carbon to form organic compounds. Plants are autotrophs, which means that they meet their carbon requirements solely from carbon dioxide in the atmosphere, or from water in the case of water-dwelling plants. Animals, being heterotrophs, are unable to make their own organic molecules and so must take them in ready-made by eating plants and other animals. Many of the more obvious differences between plants and animals result from this basic difference. For example, animals are generally mobile because they need to catch prey or graze, whereas a sessile lifestyle is adequate for a plant's requirements. Despite the

fact that we rarely see mushrooms running around the fields looking for something to eat, fungi, like animals, are heterotrophs. Their mobility comes from tiny spores. As each short-lived generation uses up its food source, the spores that will form the next generation are cast to the winds to find new food sources.
Tony Jobbins, Chipping Sodbury, Bristol.

QUESTION: My colleague can drink pints of Guinness until the cows come home, without having to empty his bladder. However, if he strays into lager quaffing, it goes straight through him. Explanation, anyone?

□ GUINNESS is good for you but lager refreshes the parts other beers cannot reach.
Jason Kilby, Rhymney, Gwent.

□ GUINNESS has the same consistency as Liffey water, of which it is supposedly made. Perhaps it also possesses the same rate of flow.
N. T. J. Kelly, Castleknock, Co. Dublin.

□ THE questioner's colleague clearly 'reacts' to Guinness. I suspect that he suffers from a number of other chronic symptoms such as migraine, nasal symptoms, joint pains, mood changes, etc. What is happening is that when he drinks Guinness (and his body reacts to it) he tends to retain fluid – this is a common symptom of food intolerance. As a result, he doesn't have to empty his bladder for some time afterwards. However, when he drinks lager this brew presumably does not upset him. I have seen quite a large number of patients who complain of fluid retention after consuming certain foods, and this is more common than most people realise. The result of fluid retention is a marked weight gain which lasts between 12 and 48 hours before returning to normal. The simple answer is to accept that Guinness upsets him and to avoid it.

(Dr) D. J. Maberly, Consultant Physician, Airedale General Hospital, Keighley, W. Yorks.

□ THE high dextrin content of Guinness could possibly be the cause of the water retention described by Dr D. J. Maberly. These soluble starch-like molecules, responsible for the beverage's body and creamy head, could, if they survived digestion and entered the bloodstream, play havoc with the body's water balance until broken down to glucose. It would be interesting to know whether others, besides the questioner's drinking mate, have made similar observations.

Dave Headey, Faringdon, Oxon.

QUESTION: If I say 'I always tell lies', am I telling the truth?

□ THE human race is made up of three types of person: saints who always tell the truth, devils who always tell lies and sinners who sometimes tell the truth and sometimes tell lies. Logically a saint cannot say 'I always tell lies' since this would be a lie. A devil cannot logically say 'I always tell lies' since this would be the truth. Only a sinner can logically say 'I always tell lies', and this would be a lie.

L. Leckie, Salford.

□ THIS is known as the Liar's Paradox. It has been around for several millennia and is usually attributed to Epimenides the Cretan, who said 'All Cretans are liars'. The quick answer is that while the question is valid from a grammatical viewpoint, from a logical point of view it is contrived contradictory nonsense. As the question is logically mean-ingless, any attempted answer would be meaningless also.

Mike Wallace, Glasgow.

☐ THIS is essentially the same as the dilemma faced by the barber who shaves all the men who don't shave themselves. The question is: who shaves the barber? Clearly he cannot shave himself because he only shaves those who don't shave themselves. However, he cannot remain unshaven as he would then have to shave himself. Logicians call this a circular argument or problem to which there is no solution. I therefore suggest that the questioner tells the truth all the time, so that the problem doesn't arise in future.
Gerard McEvoy, Bedford.

☐ GERARD McEvoy compares this with the so-called circular argument of the barber who shaves all men who don't shave themselves. The answer to the question 'Who shaves the barber?' is surely: 'No one. She doesn't shave.'
Mike Ashton, Welshpool, Powys.

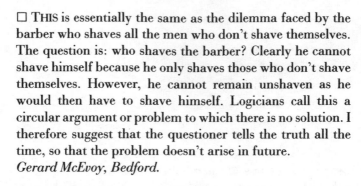

☐ BERTRAND Russell relates in his autobiography that he spent the summers of 1903 and 1904 trying to solve this contradiction, wandering the common at night and staring at a blank sheet of paper by day.
Frank Cummins, Warley, W. Midlands.

QUESTION: My computer's clock thinks the year 2000 will be a leap year. I have a nasty feeling that it is not. Am I right?

☐ THE computer is correct — 2000 will be a leap year. We need leap years because the length of the year is not a whole number of days. In fact it equals 365.2422 days; in a calendar we choose a mixture of years with 365 and 366 days to give an average close to this. In the Julian calendar, introduced by Julius Caesar, every fourth year is a leap year, making the average length of a year 365.25 days. Leap years are those with numbers divisible by four; so, for example, 1992 is a leap year. Since 1752, the more accurate

king. Large parts of the earl|ch as overtime working
explains why King Cole was|l to health. Jobs carry-
tion into the legend can be f|ore commonly done by
Heroes of Britain (Thames |ls of health-damaging
Eric L. Fitch, Burnham, Bu|(age 65 compared with
tant factor in reducing

□ THERE is a French song:
Qu'on nommait le vieux roi *wicks.*
pipette et mon vin! / Violon
Chou means 'cabbage'. So ost important influence
Could King Cole be 'Le vie|ous reduction of death
Alan Carlton Smith, Cambr|100 years. Historically,
rs, and both in agricul-
s and nuns lived to a
QUESTION: Why, in ge|n of whether too much
than men?|t men work longer hours
women have less leisure
□ EVIDENCE suggests that |most of the work in the
with a higher infant mortali|ob. It is also an error to
a better genetic resistance |ls of responsibility are
process of gender role soc|es. of production-line
likely to be brought up to |tasks can produce high
and smoke more, they are |an interview with the
risks, are less careful in wh|anniversary (when both
to show their emotions as |his longevity to 'hard
outlet for stress. Women |vere teetotal Methodists
themselves' more than men|ryone would want to go
doctors, which may mean
Men generally live more ha
more dangerous occupation
likely to be done by men an
of industrial accidents and|**of the logo on tins of**
more likely to do the dange|**be a dead lion with**
ladders and climbing on t
majority of car drivers an
1990) and are therefore m|f the notorious Israelite
accidents. Men are more lik|hich at one time every

schoolchild would have known. This rather unsavoury character became engaged to a Philistine dolly-bird (not Delilah this time). On his way to chat her up, he tore apart a young lion which was only minding its own business and roaring, as lions do, at passing strangers. On his return, Samson noticed that a swarm of bees had taken up residence in the lion's carcass and was producing honey. He scoffed some of the honey and took some more to his parents, no doubt as a sweetener, because he wanted them to arrange his marriage to this unsuitable foreigner. At his wedding celebrations, Samson seemed determined to pick a quarrel with his new in-laws. He bet them 30 designer fashion outfits that they could not find the answer to a riddle: 'Out of the eater came forth meat, and out of the strong came forth sweetness.' This foxed the Philistines completely until they persuaded Samson's new bride to use all her feminine wiles to entice the solution out of him. When the Philistines told him the answer – 'What is sweeter than honey? What is stronger than a lion?' – Samson realised that his bride had been up to no good and complained: 'If ye had not plowed with my heifer, ye had not found out my riddle.' But he had to pay up. To obtain the clothes, Samson slaughtered 30 Philistines. This put an end to the marriage. His bride then became the wife of his best (Philistine) friend. The motto 'Out of the strong came forth sweetness' can be found under the lion and bees on the tins of Golden Syrup.

Linda Holmes, Cottingham, N. Humberside. (Thanks to 144 other readers for contributions on this topic.)

□ THE Bible story about the lion and the bees is probably wrong. A local naturalist, Austin Brackenbury, reckons they weren't bees but hoverflies. These creatures, like houseflies, are attracted to rotting meat. They take many forms, mimicking other insects, such as bees and wasps. This seems a more plausible answer. Would bees, which live on nectar, set up a nest in rotting meat?

Andrew Vevers, Sheffield.

☐ AS THE person whose theory was quoted by Andrew Vevers, may I add that in ancient times certain species of hoverfly could have used the liquefying carcasses of large dead animals as a site for their aquatic larvae, which may explain the Roman poet Virgil's recipe for the spontaneous generation of hive bees from a decomposing ox. As such carcasses are not now so readily available the flies use nutrient-rich standing water. Virgil had observed the so-called drone-fly, *Eristalis tenax*, a hive bee mimic, emerging from his ox and had been mistaken (*Insect Natural History*, A. D. Imms, Collins New Naturalist). Regarding Samson's riddle, lion, bees and honey (Judges 14: 5, 8, 14), bees could have utilised the dehydrated carcass or skeleton of his lion as a nest site but, when illustrated, would this sell food? Incidentally, adult hoverflies are flower visitors and not attracted to rotting meat.
Austin Brackenbury, Sheffield.

QUESTION: In the 1980s someone designed a wooden car, which I think was called the Africar. What happened to it?

☐ AFTER experiencing the roads of Africa, and recognising the inadequacy of vehicles designed for Western consumers and smooth tarmac, Anthony Howarth developed the idea of a car designed to be used and built in Africa. This meant a reappraisal of suspension and transmission specifications and the design of a simple chassis and body, using locally produced materials such as timber and a minimum of steel. Howarth's father had observed the construction of laminated plywood airframes for Mosquito fighters and Horsa gliders during the 1939–45 war, and this influenced him. The Africar range had both four- and six-wheeled chassis with enclosed and pick-up bodies. It was all very practical and realistic, although the proposed 'boxer' two-stroke engine with supercharger was an additional problem for an

under-funded venture and was bound to involve huge investment. Africar eventually set up production on an industrial estate owned by Lancaster City Council. It produced a brochure, a copy of which I have, offering the range of Africars for sale with Citroën engines and transmissions while Howarth's dream engine was developed. But I understand that in 1988 Lancaster City Council forced the company into receivership.
J. E. Bradshaw, Warwick.

□ I MUST correct an error in the reply by Mr J. E. Bradshaw. He suggests that the company set up to manufacture the Africar was forced into receivership by Lancaster City Council in 1988. This was not the case. The city council gave considerable support to the Africar project during the three years that the company was operational. However, Africar failed to attract the very substantial level of funding that was required and eventually built up severe debts. The company finally laid off its workforce and asked the city council to repossess the premises. Following a winding-up order by a creditor, the Official Receiver was called in. Three prototype vehicles were featured in a four-part TV series shown on Channel Four, entitled *A Car for Africa*. One of these prototypes was bought by the Lakeland Motor Museum and is on display at Holker Hall, Cumbria (tel. 05395 58509).
W. Pearson, Town Clerk and Chief Executive, Lancaster.

□ THE only six-wheeled version to be built is still in perfect running order and kept at the premises of Abco UK Ltd, Mather Road, Bury, Greater Manchester.
C. A. Haines, Bacup, Lancs.

QUESTION: Who were the Weathermen?

□ THEY were a group of young revolutionaries in Greenwich

Village who took their name from Bob Dylan's song 'Subterranean Homesick Blues': 'You don't need a weatherman to know which way the wind blows.' In June 1968, they produced a document that announced that young Americans must accept the need for armed struggle. Their credo was: 'Kill all the rich people. Break up their cars and apartments. Bring the revolution home, kill your parents, that's where it's really at.' After fights with Mayor Daley's police on the streets of Chicago, they decided – at a 'war council' in Flint, Michigan, in December 1969 – to go underground and become urban guerrillas. The Weather People, as they later called themselves, because of the number of women in their ranks, were led by Bernadine Dohrn. On the morning of 5 March, 1970, Diana Oughton, Kathy Boudin, Terry Robbins, Ted Gold and Cathy Wilkerson gathered in the basement of an elegant town house at 18 West 11th Street, next door to the home of Dustin Hoffman, to make bombs. Hoffman, who had been working at his antique desk all morning, left the house at 11.30. About 45 minutes later three huge explosions went off, the force of which blew Hoffman's desk through a hole in the wall. He would certainly have been killed instantly had he still been at it. The explosions were caused by one of the group having attached a wire to the wrong terminal. Robbins, Oughton and Gold were killed; Wilkerson and Boudin, the latter totally naked, stumbled into the street and were taken in by a neighbour. The two young women quickly washed and dressed before taking flight, not to surface again for over a decade. Boudin was finally arrested in October 1981 while fleeing from an armed robbery.

Ronald Bergan, Author of Dustin Hoffman *(Virgin Books)*, *St Albans, Herts.*

QUESTION: Author and title, please, of a book I once read which offers an alternative view of the events portrayed in *The Wind in the Willows*.

□ THE questioner may have in mind *Wild Wood* by Jan Needle. It describes the uprising of the impoverished and oppressed Wild Wooders against the effete, luxurious and selfish River Bankers: the stupid and profligate Toad; the idle and dreamy Rat; the priggish, sycophantic social-climber Mole; and the class traitor Badger (of the Wood, but preferring his rich friends of the River Bank). The uprising is briefly successful, and Toad Hall becomes Brotherhood Hall, until the revolution is sold out from within, collapses and its ringleaders end up as River Bankers themselves, while the majority of the Wild Wooders revert to poverty and servitude.

J. Mackinlay, Chorlton-cum-Hardy, Manchester.

□ MY FAVOURITE character in the alternative version is a Trotskyist weasel named Boddington. He is described as being 'a strange yellow colour, thin and extraordinarily bitter' – probably a joke which only goes down well in places served by the Manchester brewery of that name.

George Crossley, Horton Bank, Bradford.

□ *WILD Wood* was published by Andre Deutsch in 1981 (ISBN 0 2339 7346 X). There is also a paperback edition published by Magnet (ISBN 0 4162 1520 3).

C. E. Morden, Great Yarmouth, Norfolk.

QUESTION: When experts on the BBC's *Antiques Road Show* value objects, they often say 'It's worth £x, but insure it for £y'. The value of y invariably exceeds x. Can anyone explain this apparent incitement to defraud the insurance companies?

□ THE figures £x and £y refer to open-market and replacement values, respectively. When valuing an object, the valuer must consider the price the owner would be able to achieve should he or she choose to sell the item on the open market at auction or to an antique dealer, for example. When valuing an item for insurance purposes, the valuer must consider the cost and possible difficulty involved in replacing the item: the owner would have to venture into the retail market where prices would reflect the incumbent over-heads and profit margins. This is certainly no incitement to defraud insurance companies but a realistic replacement valuation.

Rachel Morrish, Incorporated Society of Valuers and Auctioneers, London SW1.

QUESTION: Plants absorb oxygen at night. Is the amount absorbed sufficient to justify removing them from a bedroom at night?

□ PEOPLE absorb oxygen at night, too. Since the amount absorbed by a plant is tiny compared to that absorbed by a human bedfellow, it seems a mite unfair to banish plants but not humans from the bedroom at night.

J. D. Briggs, Nailsworth, Glos.

QUESTION: Am I entitled to my opinion?

□ YOUR entitlement to your opinion is directly proportional to your ability to justify it.

Robin Boyes, Scarborough, N. Yorks.

□ IT DEPENDS firstly on what your opinion is and secondly on what you want to do with it. The general rule, laid down in 1765, is that everything is permitted except that which is expressly prohibited: nobody may interfere with the holding or expressing of your opinions without specific authority. Thus it could be said that you are entitled to your opinion, even though there is no specific positive legal right to this effect. The difficulty with this, however, is of course that

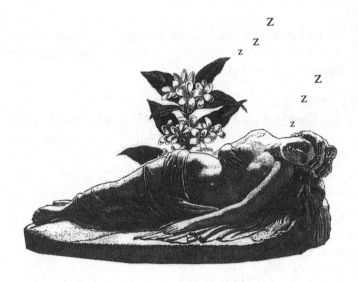

there are now several encroachments upon your 'liberty of opinion' – hence the qualified answer. You may not, for example, incite racial hatred. Neither may you blaspheme. Conversely, however, neither do you have the protection of the law against blasphemy unless you happen to belong to the correct culture or happen to hold the right religious convictions. So it's all right to ridicule some opinions or convictions (such as Islam) but not others. Fans of Bills of Rights have yet to explain which opinions they would wish to see protected by such provisions as 'everyone has the right to freedom of thought, conscience and religion' as found in the European Convention.

Adam Tomkins, Lecturer in Law, King's College London.

□ YOU are entitled to your opinion so long as you voice it as an opinion and not as knowledge. Plato's opinion, as expressed in Book VII of *The Republic* and *Parmenides*, is that knowledge is certain and infallible, and therefore cannot, logically, be mistaken. Opinion can not only be mistaken but is necessarily so, since it assumes the reality of appearance. Thus, it is possible for there to be many opinions about one thing but only one truth. Plato could, of course, be wrong but who am I to argue with the Master?

Ruth B. Whalley, Hest Bank, Lancaster.

QUESTION: What margin of accuracy would Roald Amundsen have had in reaching the South Pole?

□ AMUNDSEN and his companions travelled from their base hut to the Pole by ski, with sledges pulled by Greenland husky dogs. A sledgemeter attached to the sledge measured the miles travelled. If they travelled in a straight line (along the same line of latitude) that would have been helpful. Of course, detours were inevitable – particularly going up the mountains to reach the polar plateau. Amundsen steered by compass and this could correct the detours. It was, though, essential to fix his position by reference to the position of the Sun. For this he used a sextant with an artificial horizon (that is, a tray of mercury to reflect the image of the Sun). He also took silvered glass with a spirit bubble in case the mercury froze. At the South Pole the average position of the Sun is overhead during a complete revolution of the Earth. He therefore took a series of altitudes of the Sun over a 24-hour period (he and his men took these observations in six-hour shifts on a two-man basis, with each verifying the other's observations). To make sure they were at the Pole, and to allow for any error in calculation, Amundsen sent out one man 10 miles ahead and two others 10 miles each at right angles to the left and right. This 'boxing' of the Pole made sure the expedition had actually reached 90 degrees south. Further confirmation came when Captain Scott found the tent Amundsen had left at the Pole.

Leif Mills, West Byfleet, Surrey.

□ THE excellent reply above contains one inaccuracy. Studies of the precise observations made in sunny weather by the five fit navigators in Amundsen's team and the hasty observations of Scott's one starving navigator in poor weather have confirmed the accuracy of Amundsen's work – and also that Scott never quite got to the South Pole. Scott mistook the Norwegian tent site, pitched before observations were made, as being at the South Pole and did not continue south for a mile or two to where the Norwegian flag was raised at the actual Pole. Scott's brave incompetence killed his men but his diaries, doctored for publication, saved his reputation. Seventy-five years later, the British are still obsessed with losing as graceful amateurs rather than winning professionally.

Bruce R. Maughfling, Sevenhampton, nr Andoversford, Glos.

QUESTION: Why do the bubbles of a bubble bath disappear when a bar of soap is put into the water?

☐ BUBBLE bath products are formulations of cationic (positively charged) surface active agents and bactericides. Soaps, however, are predominantly anionic (negatively charged). When the two are mixed in water (a polar solvent) the charges cancel each other out and the bubbles collapse. To prevent a scum forming, most bubble baths contain small amounts of non-ionic dispersants to keep the dirt in suspension.
G. E. Byrne and P. K. Thomas, ICI Agrochemicals, Haslemere, Surrey.

QUESTION: How far does a football travel in an average match?

☐ A PRECISE answer could be found from videotapes of a sufficiently wide range of matches, assuming the ball stayed in shot all the time. However, it hardly seems worth the hassle since we can easily make an adequate estimate on the basis of general match experience. We need to clear up a small ambiguity first. Does the question mean distance travelled only while the ball is in play? Let's allow that distance travelled after booting into the crowd should also be included. A football match lasts 90 minutes, with the referee supposedly making allowances for stoppages before blowing the whistle at the end of each half. So, we can solve the problem if we can make a satisfactory estimate of the average speed of the ball during a match. Not so simple, perhaps, but it really depends on how precise an answer we need. During any match the speed of the ball varies from more-or-less stationary (all too often!) to significantly faster than a rapid running speed. What's a plausible average? My estimate would be about eight miles per hour. This gives a total distance travelled in a match of about 12 miles. A

rough value, no doubt, but I am confident that it is correct to within a factor of two or so – i.e. the distance travelled will be in the range 6–24 miles. Finally, my best guess is that the distance travelled by the ball in an average English Football League match is at the top end of this range, but at the bottom end in a Continental match.
Stephen J. Moss, Sutton Coldfield, W. Midlands.

QUESTION: Is there a significant difference between the nutritional requirements of dogs and cats? If I feed my young tom cat on Pedigree Chum, will he eventually turn up his toes?

☐ HE WILL eventually turn up his toes no matter what he is fed on.
N. Ashton, Neston, S. Wirral, Cheshire.

☐ A CAT will not thrive on any proprietary brand of dog food. Whereas dogs have catholic feeding habits and can subsist on low-protein or even meat-free diets, cats are necessarily carnivores and require relatively large amounts of animal protein. In addition, cats have other unique dietary needs. For example they require the aminosulphonic acid taurine, and are also thought to need preformed sources of niacin, vitamin A and arachidonic acid, all of which other mammals can synthesise from other components of the diet. These compounds are added to most prepared cat foods but are not usually present in sufficient quantity in dog food.
James Serpell, Dept of Clinical Veterinary Medicine, University of Cambridge.

QUESTION: Where can I buy a rubber chicken (as used by the suit of armour in *Monty Python* for bopping people over the head)?

☐ DEAD-LOOKING rubber chickens can be readily purchased in my local pet shop in Alsemberg, Belgium. You may wonder why. I have no idea.
E. Deboeck, Braine-l'Alleud, Belgium.

☐ THE Klutz Press (2121 Staunton Ct, Palo Alto, CA 94306, US) sells 'aerodynamically sound polyvinyl poultry' at $6 each, primarily for juggling purposes, but equally suitable, I am sure, for head bopping.
Rebecca Lloyd, London SW19.

QUESTION: When and why did the Christian Church stop viewing usury as a sin?

☐ NO DENOMINATION of the Christian Church has ever condoned usury, which we might define as an extortionate charge for the use of money or fungible goods, but the charging of interest is no longer regarded as usurious in all circumstances. In fact there is no direct condemnation of interest-taking in the New Testament; it is even tolerated in the Parable of the Talents. The Old Testament authority — Exodus 22:25, Leviticus 25:35, and Deuteronomy 20:19 — does not constitute a blanket ban on interest-taking, but condemns taking interest from the poor, and within the Jewish community. The taking of interest was forbidden to clerics from AD 314. It was strictly forbidden for laymen in 1179. The beginning of the end as far as the total ban on interest was concerned came in the sixteenth century. Although Luther and Zwingli still condemned it utterly, Calvin and some progressive Catholic thinkers such as Colet and Antoine argued that interest-taking did not constitute usury, as long as it represented the real difference between the values of present and future sums of money, and was not mere extortion. The Catholic Church still forbids usury, meaning extortionate charges, providing penalties in c2354 of the Code of Canon Law, but this does not mean that all interest-taking is sinful. The Vatican itself invests in interest-bearing schemes, and requires Church administrators to do likewise. That all interest was not in itself sinful was finally decided in a series of decisions in the institutions of the Catholic Church in the nineteenth century.

Gwen Seabourne, London N4.

☐ I DON'T think Gwen Seabourne should be allowed to get away with her anodyne answer. That the Christian Church banned usury for many centuries is not invalidated by reference to the Bible (family planning is not disallowed in the Bible). Nor can usury be defined as the extortionate charging of interest: usury is the charging of any interest. The Vatican ties itself up in complex circumlocutions to divert attention from the fact that it runs capitalist institutions based on the most blatant condoning of usury. The verbal acrobatics testify to the contradictory situation it finds itself in. Usury – all usury – is banned by Christian doctrine, as it is by Muslim doctrine. In the late Middle Ages the problem of financing the royal exchequer and setting up capitalist institutions in the face of the Christian ban on usury was resolved by allowing Jews to act as bankers. They therefore came to be viewed as pariahs, just as cow hide tanners are pariahs in Hindu society. It was in this way that the Jewish community was able to accrue vast wealth and thereby to bring down on its head the loathing of the Christians. Hence Shylock. This enmity is still the underlying basis of modern anti-Semitism. The fact that (mainly) Jewish bankers did very well out of the collapse of free-market economics in Weimar Germany was the determining reality in the rise of Hitler and the Nazi movement. Gwen Seabourne states that the Catholic Church still forbids usury. That's good enough for me.

Jonathan Morton, London W11.

QUESTION: Why is Boutros Boutros Ghali not simply Boutros Ghali?

☐ IN THE Arab world some mothers name their sons after their husband and some fathers name their sons after their father. The UN Secretary-General's name should read 'Boutros son of Boutros from the family of Chali'. One of the younger sons of King Fahd of Saudi Arabia is named after King Fahd's father. So the young prince is known as Abdulaziz son of King Fahd son of King Abdulaziz. That makes the present monarch of Saudi Arabia father as well as son of Abdulaziz.
Syed Neaz Ahmad, London SW16.

QUESTION: Do cockroaches have any redeeming features? Given that so many of them are large and juicy, why does it appear that nothing has evolved to eat them?

☐ MOST people are only aware of cockroaches as a domestic nuisance, but under 1 per cent of the known species are domiciliary pests. However, these few species often occur in disturbingly large numbers. The remaining 3,500 or so wild-living species occupy a variety of outdoor habitats, mainly found in vegetation, under stones, among leaf-litter, etc., and also in specialised habitats such as caves and deserts. Cockroaches have changed little in appearance in 250 million years, as shown by their abundance in the fossil records of the Carboniferous period. They form a natural link in the food chain for a wide range of animals, mammals, reptiles, etc., and also arthropods, including predatory insects. Mice are known to eat cockroaches but are unlikely to be any more welcome as a natural control measure in domestic environments than are the insects themselves.
(Mrs) Judith A. Marshall BSc, Department of Entomology, The Natural History Museum, London SW7.

□ ONE of their redeeming features is that they remind you to clean your kitchen cupboards regularly.
Ann Howard, Bicester, Oxon.

□ WHILE serving in a tramp-ship in the late Forties, we put in at Suez to be fumigated. After buckets of cockroaches were removed from the galley and crew's quarters, the port health authorities informed the Old Man that cockroaches were full of protein and delicious when roasted.
Ray McMahon, Southampton.

□ BEFORE the genetic engineers set to work on producing something that eats cockroaches, can I ask them to develop a predator for dogs? They are considerably larger and juicier than cockroaches, yet have even fewer redeeming features.
Geoff Black, Cambridge.

QUESTION: My daughter has acquired Wet Wet Wet's latest album in cassette form. After two playings, the tape severed. All it needs is sticking together again, but the case appears to be unopenable. Solutions, please.

□ THE case may appear to be unopenable, but it will split in half with enough persuasion. However, it is extremely un-likely that it will be closable again afterwards. If so, buy a blank cassette which can be unscrewed. Remove the screws and take the cassette apart, taking care to note the path of the tape around the guides and runners inside the case. Then remove the spools and all the tape. Break open the Wet Wet Wet cassette (this may be a more pleasurable experience than actually listening to it), making sure that you do not inflict any more damage to the tape itself. Cut away any damaged or stretched pieces of tape, and carefully repair the tape with a thin piece of Sellotape (don't use too much or it will jam). Now take the two tape spools from the Wet Wet Wet cassette and put them in the case of the other cassette.

Thread the tape correctly and put the cassette back together with the Wet Wet Wet tape inside. Unfortunately, this solution results in the waste of a perfectly good blank cassette, but is considerably cheaper than replacing the whole thing.
Paul Vallis, Bristol.

□ DON'T dare try to repair it! Take it back to the supplier and demand a replacement. You will be letting the rest of us down if you don't. The sooner we all refuse to accept faulty products as a nation, the better off we'll all be.
Paul Nation, Ruislip, Middx.

QUESTION: It is often asserted that New Yorkers responded to the 1965 power failure by going to bed and having sex, resulting in a significant increase in the birth rate nine months later. An urban myth, or is there evidence to support this?

□ THE story of a baby boom following nine months after any kind of catastrophe is so good that it recurs every so often. It was reported that large numbers of copulating couples were discovered preserved in the ashes of Pompeii. Rises in births were reported nine months after Pearl Harbor and nine months after the out'break of the Korean War. After the 10-day blackout of August 1966, the *New York Times* reported a sharp increase in births in six New York hospitals. The story spread rapidly round the world, but it was five years before Richard Urdy, a statistician, demonstrated that the birth rate over the period in question was no greater than that of the same period in other years between 1951 and 1969. Mr Urdy vanished into obscurity, but the story has refused to die. In 1967 Chicago maternity hospitals prepared for 'an avalanche of snow babies' nine months after the massive snowfall of the preceding winter. It never materialised. On 14 July 1977, New York City had another blackout. The resultant stories of frantically busy maternity hospitals were given even greater credence by being the subject of Alistair Cooke's *Letter from America*. On that occasion the NY Dept of Health reported births as 9,088 in March 1978; 8,278 in April; 8,900 in May. In November 1979 the story re-emerged in Britain following an 11-week ITV dispute. On that occasion I tried hard to track down the source of the story and the names of the 'experts', ranging from a 'BMA spokesman' to a 'prominent sociologist' who had commented. All the journalists involved proved coy about their sources.

John Peniket, Churchdown, Glos.

QUESTION: Those railway trucks propelled by two people pumping a handle up and down, and seen only in films, seem to be the most green form of transport. Do they still exist; were they hard work; did you hire or buy them?

☐ THE trolleys, usually known as handcars, were once widely used in North America and other countries where track maintenance crews had to travel several miles to work. They were rare in Britain, but I believe a few were used in the Scottish Highlands. The combination of energetic movement and opportunity for thrilling escapades endeared them to early silent-film makers. Several railway museums own examples, and races are staged from time to time. The most ambitious handcar journey was organised in Australia in 1988, when a standard-gauge, four-person handcar was pumped about 2,700 miles from Perth to Sydney via Adelaide. It was powered by teams of railway employees and enthusiasts, working in relays, and averaged about 70 miles a day for some 39 days. Handcars do not involve much effort. Just push-start it, jump on and pump to keep it rolling. My own experience is on level track in warm climates. If, however, the questioner is considering taking

advantage of Nicholas Ridley's proposal to allow any opera-
tor on to Britain's railways, the climb from Bridge of Allen to
Druimuachdar in the teeth of a north-easterly gale may
prove a little difficult. For these conditions I recommend the
Indian Railways' track inspector's trolley, which is equipped
with a comfortable chair, sunshade or umbrella, and two
barefoot pushers. Just as green, and a provider of employ-
ment as well.
Mike Swift, Huddersfield, W. Yorks.

□ PUMP trolleys still exist on many preserved railways,
including one on the Dean Forest Railway in Gloucester-
shire. Although fairly hard to start, for the reasonably fit
they are easy to propel once an initial momentum has been
achieved. Stopping is possibly the most difficult aspect; an
emergency stop is impossible.
*David Ponter, Dean Forest Railway, Staunton, nr
Gloucester.*

**QUESTION: Given that a young kangaroo spends some
months in its mother's pouch, how does the mother
clean out the excrement and detritus that must
accumulate?**

□ AS EVERY schoolchild knows, kangaroos live in the Anti-
podes, where everything walks upside down. Their pouches
are cleared out by gravity.
Bob Frost, Deal, Kent.

□ THE answer depends on the age of the young kangaroo, or
joey. If the joey has not left the mother's pouch she cleans it
using her paws and tongue without disturbing the joey.
When the joey is mature enough it starts to leave the pouch
for short periods – which gives the mother time to clean out
her pouch as much as she'd like until the joey wants to

return. This is in contrast to the popular belief that the mother absorbs the excrement back into her body.
Craig Little, Caloundra, Queensland, Australia.

QUESTION: What was the name of the Queen of Sheba?

□ THE Bible (1 Kings 10 and 2 Chronicles 9) is silent on this question, as it is on the location of Sheba itself. Arab tradition calls her Bilqis, and identifies her kingdom with the ancient Saba, in what is now Yemen. Many scholars accept this. Some credence, however, should be given to the case of Ethiopia, on the opposite shore of the Red Sea: an ancient Christian outpost which had close contacts with Judaism and biblical Israel. Ethiopia claims the Queen of Sheba for its own and calls her 'Makeda', linking her with the civilisation based on the ancient city of Axum, in what is now Tigre province. This attribution is central to Ethiopia's historical identity, even to this day. The Ethiopic work, the *Kebra-Nagast* ('Glory of Kings'), greatly elaborates on the Old Testament story. In it we are told that Solomon seduced Makeda through a ruse. The result of this physical union was the birth of Menelik I, founder of the Solomonic line of Ethiopia and the blood-link upon which, over ensuing centuries, contenders to the Ethiopian throne had to base their claims. The last incumbent of the Solomonic dynasty was Haile Selassie, overthrown in the Marxist revolution of 1974 when a link between Ethiopia and the House of Israel that stretched back almost 3,000 years was abruptly severed. Another interesting aspect of the *Kebra-Nagast* account is Menelik's surreptitious removal from the Temple of Jerusalem of the original Ark of the Covenant, containing the stone tablets of the law that were given to Moses in Sinai. A replica was left in its place. It is claimed that the Ark survives to this day, and that it is in the sanctuary of the Cathedral of St Mary of Zion in Axum where it may be seen only by those few priests who are appointed to guard it.
Stephen Bell, Newark, Notts.

QUESTION: Is American rice grown in paddy fields as it is in South-East Asia?

□ YES, but in Arkansas the rice seed is often sown by helicopter in fields artificially irrigated from fast-flowing canal waters looped about the land and dug by modern machinery.
Stephen O'Sullivan, Dun Laoghaire, Co. Dublin, Ireland.

□ NOT all South-East Asian rice is grown as padi. I have a friend who has a rice field at the highest point of his hill farm in the Philippines. Upland rice is thought to have a better flavour than padi.
John Atkins, Birch, Colchester.

QUESTION: The Romans presumably used olive oil in their lamps. I cannot make this work, even in a Roman lamp. How did they do it?

□ I AM writing with an olive oil lamp burning beside me. It was made for me by a potter friend to use in history teaching, but is not an exact copy of ancient lamps. It uses a specialist wick, and I think that the wick may be the critical factor. I did have some problems at first. The wick needs to be soaked in the oil before lighting and the flame needs to be close enough to the oil to maintain the supply by capillary action. This means constant topping up, which is probably why ancient lamps are.so small: it isn't the total amount of oil in the reservoir that is important but its height. Mine has a large reservoir and the wick hole is high relative to the reservoir opening, so to avoid waste of expensive oil I top it up with water, which may seem odd but it works.
Penelope Stanford, Greenhithe, Kent.

QUESTION: What makes white chocolate white and why is it called chocolate?

☐ COCOA paste, cocoa butter, sugar and milk are the four basic ingredients for making chocolate. By blending them in accordance with specific recipes the three types of chocolate are obtained: 1, plain chocolate (cocoa paste, cocoa butter and sugar); 2, milk chocolate (cocoa paste, cocoa butter, sugar and milk); 3, white chocolate (cocoa butter, sugar and milk). Cocoa as a drink was first introduced into Britain during the seventeenth century but the Aztec Indians in Central America had been consuming bitter drinking chocolate, called *chocolatl*, hundreds of years earlier. Don Cortez, the Spanish explorer, is said to have drunk a thick chocolate drink out of a goblet with the Aztec emperor, Montezuma. Cortez took cocoa beans with him back to Spain so that he could make a thick chocolate drink. Chocolate for eating was not known until early Victorian times.
Nicole Stalker, Public Relations Consultant to the Biscuit, Cake, Chocolate and Confectionery Alliance, London WC1.

QUESTION: I recently came across a book of instruction for Aulay Macaulay's shorthand, published in 1747 and described as 'an universal character fitted to all languages'. Who was Aulay Macaulay and does anyone use his shorthand today?

☐ HE WAS a tea merchant who lived in St Ann's Square, Manchester, and was also based at Cateaton Street, London. He was possibly the owner of Manchester's first theatre. Along with his other wares, he regularly puffed his shorthand in the local press. His first system, Polygraphy, appeared in 1747. He made bold claims for its superiority, applying it to Dutch, French, Greek, Hebrew, Latin, Spanish and Welsh, and providing witnesses that a boy of seven was able to write it after only four lessons. Though Macaulay was not a professional shorthand teacher – the book was marketed as obviating the need for personal tuition, doubtless to undercut rivals – he offered his services to the upper classes of London at a guinea a session. He tried to interest the early Methodists in the system and by 1756 boasted 1,500 subscribers. 'Improvements' in a third edition that year (in effect a separate system) were published around 1760 as *The New Short-Hand*. Macaulay's systems had serious flaws; their deliberate shunning of rudimentary phonetic principles made them unsuitable for rapid writing and doomed them to be overshadowed. Several manuscripts in Macaulay survive, including an attractive transcription of Pope's poems, and I'd be delighted to hear from readers possessing manuscripts in Macaulay or any other eighteenth-century system. Macaulay had nineteenth-century adherents but I know of no proficient users today. I attempted the basics two years ago but found progress tortuously slow.

Timothy Underhill, Pembroke College, Cambridge.

QUESTION: Could anyone recommend a humane mouse trap for catching the mouse alive to release it away from the house?

☐ YES. Go to a good (i.e. old-fashioned) ironmonger and for £2.50 or less you can obtain Trip Trap ('The Friendly Mousetrap') from Petcraft. The instructions are in three languages but only the English version says: 'We advise that the Trip Trap be checked regularly to minimise stress to the trapped mouse.' Are the British extra sensitive or extra thick?

Irene Palmer, Portsmouth, Hants.

☐ WE HAVE used the Trip Trap very successfully in a country cottage. I bought ours from a local pet shop. It was supplied with easy-to-follow instructions but I would add three more. Drill a hole in the end of the trap where the mouse's nose

faces, to ensure that it gets enough air. Use a piece of chocolate as bait (we found mice prefer it to anything else). Lastly, if you release the mouse near the house it will quickly find a way back in.
Anne Canham, Carlisle.

☐ A LONGWORTH mammal trap (used on numerous field studies trips) will catch a mouse or any other small mammal so that it can be released elsewhere. But beware. In my experience, the mouse often bites the hand that frees it.
(Dr) Susan Burr, Principal Teacher of Biology, Kyle Academy, Ayr.

☐ MY FATHER'S infallible mousetrap was a tin box, the lid held on by a rubber band but propped open by a Twiglet. When the mouse ate through the Twiglet it was caught.
(Mrs) Rosy Hunt, York. (Thanks for information – and a mousetrap – from 73 humane readers.)

QUESTION: I have been told that if battleships of the Second World War era fired a broadside with all the guns of their main armament at the same time they would capsize. Can this be true?

☐ THE questioner has been listening to old sailors telling tall sea stories. While it is true that a full broadside loosed by a Second World War battlewagon would send considerable shock waves reverberating through the ship itself, shaking the inmates, bending the odd fitting or two and scattering unsecured articles hither and thither, that would be all. The latter-day dreadnought was somewhat akin to an iceberg. In normal practice full broadsides were seldom discharged. Salvoes (i.e. the firing of alternate guns from the same turret) were quicker and created less smoke, allowing more rapid spotting of fall of shot. More often than not, technical problems with the weaponry, particularly with the 14-inch

Mk VIII mounted by the King George V class, precluded the
simultaneous use of all barrels. Nevertheless, there were
occasions when Royal Navy battleships administered the
'full dose' during the Second World War. For example, HMS
Rodney to the *Bismarck* and the *Warspite* and *Valiant* to the
Italian heavy cruisers at the Battle of Matapan. The *Duke of
York* fired at least one 10-gun broadside at the *Scharnhorst*
at the Battle of the North Cape in 1943. In all those cases,
however, it was the recipient rather than the deliverer of the
broadside that did the capsizing.
Peter N. Lonsdale, Birkenhead, Merseyside.

☐ IN FILM footage of the Vietnam War, USS *New Jersey* is
seen firing a full broadside of nine 16-inch guns in shore
bombardment (a role that was performed with great accuracy in the Gulf War). A battleship will not capsize but will
move about six feet sideways due to the recoil of her guns –
the water acts like a buffer. However, I understand that the
Nelson class of British First World War battleships, which
had three 16-inch turrets forward of the bridge and nothing
behind, were unable to fire their front two guns within
30 degrees of the bow because of the risk of putting the stern
under and sinking. Could someone confirm my suspicion?
Will Denham, Shrewsbury, Shropshire.

☐ BATTLESHIPS have fired full broadsides on a number of
occasions, as one of your correspondents noted, although the
other correspondent who believed he had seen a ship move
six feet sideways on film is certainly mistaken. The propel-
lant necessary to throw nine 1½-ton shells a distance of 20
miles, leaving the gun barrels at 1,700 mph, exerted a shock
load of several hundred tons to the mountings of the ship but
even this could not move 57,000 tons of inertia, let alone
shift a similar mass of water out of the way. A great deal of
ingenious engineering absorbed this massive recoil by com-
pressing air in cylinders as the 100-ton guns jumped back a

mere 40 or so inches in about half a second. That same air pressure was then used to push the gun back into its firing position. By absorbing all the energy in this way, the ship did not heel over, as the original questioner thought. However, the blast of the propellent gases escaping from the barrel when the projectile left became a shock wave that impacted the structure of the ship, creating massive vibration and sometimes ripping up deck planking, fracturing steel fittings and even causing hull plates to flex and shear off the rivets that held them together. But it was the sea spray churned up by this shock wave moving away, along the side of the ship, that caused your correspondent to think that the USS *New Jersey* had jumped sideways. It was the danger from this gun blast that stopped HMS *Rodney* from firing with her guns pointed close to her bow, not the risk of pushing her stern under water as was suggested last week. During her fight with the *Bismarck*, a salvo fired with her guns pointing a little astern of the beam blew out all the windows in the superstructure and knocked the tin hats off the bridge crew's heads. Incidentally, even the *New Jersey*'s broadside firing was not truly simultaneous. Within each three-gun turret, each barrel went off 0.06 seconds apart so that the supersonic shock waves from the shells travelling through the air did not interfere with each other and cause them to deviate from their predicted path. If you want to see big guns today, take a trip to the Imperial War Museum where two 15-inchers stand guard at the front entrance.
Sean Waddingham, Bexley, Kent.

QUESTION: What useful purpose do eyebrows serve?

☐ THEY keep actors like Roger Moore in work.
Chris Ainsworth, Ramsbottom, Lancs.

☐ IN THE absence of a headband they act as gutters to divert perspiration from the eyes (in antipodean countries they

catch tears). No doubt a higher form of life will evolve drainpipes to further the process.
Chris Jeffery, London N4.

☐ REMOVING them with a razor and then indulging in some vigorous physical exercise will confirm just how effective they really are.
Paul Vallis, Bristol.

QUESTION: How do Mr and Mrs Paul Daniels perform their baffling mind-reading act?

☐ VERY badly.
Robert Cox (member of the Magic Circle), Hemel Hempstead, Herts.

QUESTION: Why do people waste energy by filling kettles, etc., from the cold tap? Is there a health risk from using water from the hot tank?

☐ THOSE of us without instant water heaters at the sink run about six pints of water out of the tap (about two kettlefuls) before it comes hot. This water was once hot (when the tap was last turned off) but its heat has since leaked away. To fill a kettle this way, you therefore throw away twice as much energy as you use. It is similarly much more economical to wash up with hot water from the kettle. If you are worried that you may heat more than you need or that you may waste the small amount of residual heat in the body of the kettle, refill the kettle straight away to its normal level. The added cold water absorbs any remaining heat, reducing the temperature difference between the kettle and its surroundings and thus slowing the rate at which residual heat energy is lost (as I recall, the rate is proportional to the difference

between the fourth power of the absolute temperatures of the kettle and its surroundings).
David G. Poole, Whitley Bay, Tyne and Wear.

☐ THERE is a potential risk in drinking stored water if the cold tank feeding the hot cylinder is not completely covered and screened. Most tanks are not: in my work as a registered plumber I find many dead birds, mice and insects. To drink water from such sources (assuming you would still want to), it must be boiled for three minutes to kill the bacteria, so there would be no energy saving, and modern automatic kettles won't do this anyway.
Roger Bisby, Reigate, Surrey.

QUESTION: I have read that there is mathematical proof of the existence of extraterrestrial life. Unfortunately, in the same source, I read that there is mathematical proof that such life forms, had they existed, would have made contact with us by now. Any resolution of this paradox?

☐ ALTHOUGH one cannot mathematically prove the existence of extraterrestrial life, Frank Drake and Carl Sagan of Cornell University have estimated the number of technologically advanced civilisations in the galaxy by calculating the product of the following factors (using very conservative estimates for their values): the number of stars in the galaxy, the fraction of stars having planetary systems, the number of planets in such a system which are ecologically suited for life, the fraction of suitable planets on which life actually arises, the fraction of such planets on which intelligent life arises, the fraction of these planets on which a technical civilisation develops and the fraction of a planet's lifetime for which a technical civilisation exists. This last is the most difficult to estimate; if we assume that it is common for civilisations to destroy themselves, then they will last for about one-millionth of a per cent of the lifetime of the planet (as we have so far). In this case the estimate for the number of technical civilisations in our galaxy is about 10. Alternatively, if we assume that civilisations commonly survive, then this number is of the order of millions. As for the second part of the question, again, there can be no mathematical proof. We must assume they are capable of contacting us but do not want to. Perhaps it is imperative that we reach a particular stage of development without being certain of the existence of life elsewhere? Perhaps they are advanced enough to consider surreptitious observation of other species very rude?

Peter Ostrowski, Wickford, Essex.

QUESTION: What happens to the voting slips used in British elections after they have been counted?

☐ UNDER the Representation of the People Act 1983 the Returning Officer, usually a senior official of the local council, has to ensure that all ballot papers, counterfoils and the polling clerks' marked copies of the electoral register are safely deposited with the Clerk of the Crown in Chancery (a senior officer of the Lord Chancellor's Department). This is so that if any corrupt or illegal election practices are reported the appropriate documents are available for inspection. All such documents are supposed to be officially sealed so that there is no chance of interference by any party and, according to the 1983 Act, the seal can only be broken by the order of the High Court or Parliament itself. In practice ballot papers are simply bundled up into paper sacks and transported to a warehouse in Hayes, Middlesex, for the statutory period of one year and one day. Following the 1987 general election, I reported on the disposal of the 7,000 sacks of this 'low-grade confidential waste' for a national newspaper. The papers were transported by truck from the Hayes warehouse to be incinerated in the North

London Waste Authority plant at Enfield. During that process we witnessed dozens of sacks splitting and many hundreds of spent ballot papers spilling for all to see. This adds weight to the conspiracy theory that security around the election documents is very lax, and that the vote-tracing procedure has been used to identify people voting for fringe candidates. Votes can be traced by matching the numbered ballot paper to its similarly numbered counterfoil; the numbered counterfoil also bears the voter's registration number from the electoral register which is hand-written by the Polling Clerk when the ballot paper is issued. As all the ballot papers for each candidate – including fringe candidates such as Sinn Fein, communists, fascists, nationalists, etc. – are bundled together, anyone having access to those documents can speedily trace the name and address of every voter for such candidates if they wish. In 1981 Gordon Winter – a former agent of BOSS, the South African Secret Service – writing in his book, *Inside Boss*, claimed that the South African government knew the identity of everyone who voted for the Communist Party of Great Britain – thanks to British intelligence using this simple vote-tracing procedure. In any event, the notion that we have a secret vote is very misleading. One positive outcome of the 1987 general election, however, was that the incineration of 91 tons of ballot papers contributed to the 21 megawatts per hour output of the North London Waste Authority plant, which supplies electricity to Tottenham.

David Northmore, Author of The Freedom of Information Handbook, *London W1.*

□ I DO NOT know what happens to the voting slips for Conservative candidates, after they have been counted, but in the mid-1960s those for communists were tallied against their counterfoils in the ballot books (just like cheque books) and those who had had the temerity to vote for a communist were identified from the electoral roll. Their names were forwarded to Special Branch and to MI5, almost certainly as

a matter of routine. The source for this information was a good one. He was a postgraduate student doing his doctoral research on local government in a Midlands steel town where he was attached to the town clerk's department. One day he opened a cupboard, looking for some documents, and found instead a large number of ballot slips, all of which were marked in favour of a communist candidate in the local elections. The town clerk returned and found the student with the slips and told him (knowing the student's safely right-wing views) that it was one of his regular chores to forward the names of communist voters to the Special Branch. As the town had a strong communist tradition it was a recurrent task for the town clerk and the slips had been put to one side until he had time to deal with them. The then student (my informant) saw nothing wrong with this procedure — which made his account the more believable.
Michael Wilson, Thame, Oxon.

☐ I WAS interested to read Michael Wilson's letter about ballot papers cast for communist candidates. What he describes was not the practice everywhere in the country. In the 1950s and 1960s I was the town clerk of two Lancashire authorities where we not only had communist candidates but also communist members on the councils for short periods. While the ballot papers cast for the communist candidates were dealt with in the same way as those for other parties, it is true that police acting on behalf of the Special Branch did take an interest in these candidates. They always came to the town hall and took the names of the proposer, seconder and assentors of the communist candidates. However this information, unlike the ballot paper, is not secret and was published in an election notice.
J. W. Blomeley, Streatley-on-Thames, Berks.

☐ LIBERTY (the National Council for Civil Liberties) has long been worried about the risk to the secrecy of the ballot described by your correspondents and has proposed that

election law be reformed to make vote-tracing impossible, by removing the requirement that voters' electoral register numbers are written on the counterfoils of the ballots issued to them. Liberty would welcome information about improper vote-tracing, such as described last week in Michael Wilson's letter. He and anybody else who has information about this are invited to contact (directly or through an intermediary) Andrew Puddephatt, Liberty's General Secretary, at 21 Tabard Street, London SE1 4LA (tel: 071-403 3888).
Seamus O'Connell, London NW6.

□ TWO further questions are prompted by the letters about serial numbers on ballot papers. First, if I delete or cut off the serial number do I invalidate my vote? Second, have serial numbers ever been used for their official purpose – the investigation of electoral fraud?
Janet Johnson, Rugby, Warwicks.

□ JANET Johnson asks if serial numbers on ballot papers have ever been used for their official purpose: the investigation of electoral fraud. There was a case in the late 1970s in a council election in Richmond-upon-Thames. A German couple living in Gerard Road, Barnes, turned up to vote. They were not entitled to as they were not British citizens, but the poll clerk confused them with another family with a very similar name only two doors away, and they registered their vote. When the correct Mrs Such & Such turned up to vote she was told her name was marked as having already voted, and was allowed only a 'tendered' vote, which meant she could mark a ballot paper that was not put in the ballot box but kept separate. In the same street a girl was unwisely persuaded by a political agent to vote, although her name was marked with a 'Y' on the voting register as she had not quite reached voting age. The result of the election in our ward was extremely close, but after recounts the Conservative candidate was declared the winner with a majority of

only one or two votes. At this, the genuine voter with a German name demanded that her case be looked into. It was established that her vote was valid and her German neighbours' not. The under-age girl's vote was also ruled invalid. By means of the serial numbers of the ballot papers copied on to the voting register, the invalid papers were traced and it was discovered that all three were for the Conservative candidate. The 'tendered' vote was for the Liberal. Thus the result was to reverse the outcome of the election in our ward.
Margaret Sharp, Barnes, London SW13.

QUESTION: If you chuck a spider out of a window from a considerable height does it survive?

☐ IN HIS essay 'On Being the Right Size' (1927), J. B. S. Haldane described the effect of dropping various animals down a 1,000-yard mine shaft. A mouse (and anything smaller) on reaching the bottom 'gets a slight shock and walks away'. By comparison 'a rat is killed, a man is broken, a horse splashes'. Haldane explains that the resistance presented to movement by the air is proportional to the surface of the moving object. In a small animal or insect the resistance to falling is considerably greater than the driving force.
Peter Barnes, Milton Keynes.

QUESTION: Is it true that beards were not allowed in Albania and, if so, what was the rationale behind it?

☐ DURING the 'glorious epoch of the party' they were outlawed as an 'alien manifestation', along with rock music, cosmetics and 'extravagant clothing' such as jeans and miniskirts. The ban was part of the opposition to Western influences. Cheeks had to be shaved up to the temple, and

the cheekbone was sometimes known as *kocka e partise* (the bone of the party). Disgusted Albanians have since pointed out that the ruling had no ideological basis, and that Marx, Engels and Lenin all set personal examples with beards.
John Hodgson, Vienna, Austria.

□ BEARDS were associated with the Muslim and Orthodox Christian clergy. The public celebration of religion was forbidden in 1967, when Albania tried to follow the ideals of Mao's Cultural Revolution.
Richard Pierce, Albania Society of Britain, Chippenham, Wilts.

□ BEARDS were never illegal, merely strongly discouraged, along with long hair (in males) and other manifestations of Western-influenced individualism. However, in 1990, in an attempt to break growing dissent, the old communist regime relaxed its policy of enforced haircuts, only to send out its secret police, the dreaded '106', a few months later to round up, beat up and even 'cause to disappear' young men from all over the country who had taken advantage of what they had thought to be a genuine new-found liberalism. This trap laid by the government backfired in that it led directly to the mass exodus of mainly young people, like ourselves, who fled to Italy in January 1991.
Shpetim Lekatari, Xhovani Ziu, Ilir Koleci and Dritan Tafa, Aviano Catering School, Pordenone, nr Venice, Italy.

□ WHEN I visited Albania in 1960 we were accompanied by the Rt Hon. John Biffen. One day when we were going out on a coach he was sent back to change into long trousers because shorts were considered indecent away from the beach.
J. E. Marcer, Brockworth, Glos.

QUESTION: Given that my feet enjoy a bath as much as the rest of me, why are they the only bits that smell of mature Stilton?

☐ YOUR feet are infected with a close relative of the fungus that gives Stilton its blue veins. Washing is of no use because your footwear provides a humid, anaerobic environment which the fungus spores find irresistible. This 'bugs' Benidorm' is achieved by wearing nylon stretch socks and shoes made from impermeable synthetic materials, along with never baring your feet outside the bedroom or the bathroom. The solution is twofold. First, for immediate relief use a fungicidal foot-powder available from any chemist. Second, for a permanent solution, wear natural-fibre socks and leather shoes (which let out the sweat and let in the air) along with going barefoot or be-sandalled whenever possible. Alternatively, go into cheese-making.
Val Dobson, Bamber Bridge, Preston, Lancs.

☐ I CAN'T provide an explanation but I can offer a cheap, effective and long-lasting cure. Buy some boracic acid powder from a chemist, sprinkle a small amount on clean feet, socks, shoes, etc., for a few days. Wear leather in-soles in trainers, wellingtons, etc., at all times. This worked for me.
Dick Bergman, Guildford, Surrey.

☐ AMONG the bacteria resident on the human skin is a species named *Brevibacterium epidermis*. A related species, *Brevibacterium linens*, is actually used as a culture in, surprise, surprise, cheese making. Both species of bacteria break down long-chain fatty acids found both in milk and on skin secretions to produce the malodorous gases methane thiol and hydrogen sulphide – hence the characteristic smell. The skin of the sole of the foot contains a very high number of sweat glands which, in combination with the higher skin temperatures of a shod foot, creates a tropical

pedal micro-climate which encourages proliferation of the bacteria. In addition to the sound advice offered by Dick Bergman, I recommend natural-fibre socks or stockings (synthetics tend to aggravate the condition), changing these during the day if the feet perspire excessively, and ensuring that shoes are alternated so that the moisture accumulating inside them has at least 24 hours to evaporate.
Michael A. Nicol, Podiatry Lecturer, London W5.

QUESTION: Is it true that tapeworms were used as an aid to slimming in the 1920s? Did it work and, if so, how can I contract this parasite?

☐ I THOUGHT it was during the eighteenth century that tapeworms were used for slimming, not the 1920s. A regular diet of steak tartare should give you a good chance of becoming infested.
John Fisher, Hitchin, Herts.

☐ ARTHUR Jackson, in his book *More Tales of a Country Practice* (Souvenir Press), describes how segments of a northern Scandinavian tapeworm, *Diphyllobothrium latum*, were found in the faeces of an emaciated elderly patient. Some time before the war, she had taken 'Dr Simpson's famous simple slimming pills'. Two pills containing the flesh of a worm-infested freshwater fish were swallowed to start the slimming process and two more, presumably containing a vermicide, should have been taken when the desired weight was attained. The patient, happy to be thin, never took the antidote. The author does not name the species of fish concerned, nor does he mention whether it must be eaten raw. Perhaps a ticket to Finland would be of further help to the enquirer.
Ruth Mundy, Cornwall County Library, Redruth.

☐ AROUND 1930 a tablet was advertised as 'slimming without dieting'. It was said in letters to the press that tablets left untaken erupted and maggots crawled out.
L. Clarke, Northampton.

☐ THERE are various human tapeworms but the only one which could safely be used is the beef tapeworm. This might be contracted in France or other European countries from eating very rare beef or steak tartare, but infection could more easily be picked up in Ethiopia, where it is particularly common. However, there are many reasons why this should not be attempted. There is no evidence that it does aid slimming and the tapeworm has rather unpleasant habits best not outlined in a newspaper read over the breakfast table.
(Dr) R. Muller, St Albans, Herts.

QUESTION: Are there any authentic old maps with 'Here be dragons' or suchlike on them?

☐ 'HERE be dragons' is probably apocryphal, since few maps had English texts until the seventeenth century, when dragons were already out of fashion. Similar Latin inscriptions are quite common. The earliest appear in Ptolemy's Atlas (*c.* AD 150), warning of elephants, hippos and cannibals. Medieval *mappae mundi* ('world maps') are stuffed with such tales: people with feet so big they lie on the ground and use them as umbrellas, giant gold-mining ants, Amazons who keep men in cages – but not many dragons. It took the Renaissance to make dragon hunting an exact geographical science. Bishop Olaus Magnus's map of Scandinavia (1539) illustrates and gives copious notes on dozens of monsters and marks the caves where trolls live. As geography became more scientific, mythical creatures were the first casualty. Yet the questioner can take heart from the

words on the Atlantic chart of Admiral Piri Re'is (1513): 'Here are monsters – all harmless souls'.
Ian Seymour, March, Cambs.

☐ DURING a total of more than 50 years handling old maps we have been unable to find any with the well-known phrase – although pictures of dragons and other monsters do often appear and fanciful written descriptions abound. Martin Waldseemüller (*c.* 1470–1518), who devised the name 'America', depicted an island called 'Brazil' south west of the Shannon on the first printed modern map of the British Isles in 1513. The renowned cartographer Abraham Ortelius (1528–98), on his map of the North Atlantic, inscribed 'Pigmes hic habitant' (Pigmies live here) on the area we know as the North Polar icecap. Many later cartographers showed California as an island, perhaps predicting the possible results of earthquakes to come. For more details, see 'Here be dragons . . . myths and legends on old maps', chapter 10 of our book *Antique Maps – A Collector's Guide* (Phaidon–Christie's, 1986 and 1989) – now, alas, out of print.
Carl Moreland FRGS and David Bannister FRGS, Cheltenham, Glos.

QUESTION: Several florists have told me to put my cut flowers in lemonade instead of water. Why?

☐ THE reason lemonade can help up to a point is that flowers need nutrition in the form of sugars. Slightly raising the acidity of the water (lemonade contains citric acid) also aids water uptake. However, the big problem with lemonade is that its anti-bacterial properties are inadequate: the resulting growth of micro-organisms in the water causes blockages in flower stems and makes the blooms wilt. Sugar also helps the bacteria to multiply more quickly. On the other hand, proprietary flower foods contain all the correct ingredients in the right proportions to enable flowers to last longer. They are also cheaper than lemonade, white wine, aspirin and other popular solutions. To get the best from cut flowers, about an inch should be removed from the bottom of the stems, making a slanted cut with a sharp knife to enable the maximum uptake of water and nutrients. Remove all the leaves which would otherwise be below the water-line and place the flowers in lukewarm water already containing flower food in a scrupulously clean vase. Place the flowers in good light but away from hot direct sunlight or heat sources, and not in draughts or near ripening fruit. Top up the water as required and remove dead flower heads as they occur.

Veronica Richardson, Flowers & Plants Association, London SW8.

QUESTION: Is it true that panther racing was staged at Stamford Bridge in the 1950s?

☐ IT MIGHT have been in the 1930s rather than the 1950s, when speedway was staged there. Prewar speedway meetings were never short of gimmicks, including animal ones. For instance, promoter Johnnie Hoskins once proposed to race five cheetahs against his West Ham team, but for safety reasons the animals were not allowed to run untethered in case they ate any spectators. Also at Wembley there were attempts to introduce real lions to boost the image of the Wembley Lions speedway side – but this also appears to have been too hazardous an idea and was abandoned.

(Rev.) Michael Whawell, London EC1.

☐ PANTHER racing did take place there, but only for a few weeks in the autumn of 1951. The panthers proved to be too fast for the hare. On one occasion a panther escaped while leading a race and was last seen heading down King Street in Hammersmith at about 70 mph.

Jack Carter, Luton, Beds.

☐ IN 1938, Mr Wilson Harris, the long-serving editor of the *Spectator*, asked me, his most junior reporter, to cover a novel event at Wembley Stadium: a race between greyhounds and a cheetah. The greyhounds were given a suitable start before the cheetah was released, but it quickly overtook them. The only signs of aggression came from the greyhounds.
Richard Scott, Lagrasse, France.

QUESTION: What is the point of living?

☐ NEWCASTLE United 1, Sunderland 0.
Kriss Knights, Newcastle-upon-Tyne.

☐ TO CREATE consumer demand, without which the economy will not come out of recession and the world will end. So there.
Bob Everett, London NW2.

☐ I DON'T know, but I'm dying to find out.
Peter Reilly, Ridgwood High School, Stourbridge, Worcs.

☐ SINCE Aristotle, the 'point' of life, if there is such a thing, has been taken as being its *telos* ('end' or 'aim'). Philosophy has two sorts of answer. The first is that it is not a genuine question, because 'living', like 'swimming', but unlike 'sleeping' or 'lying', can be pursued for its own sake: it doesn't presuppose somewhere to end up, nor is it the means to some further end which is part of the meaning of the idea. So a sufficient answer to 'Why are you swimming?' can be 'Because I like it', whereas to 'Why are you eating?' it would be, for example, 'Because I'm hungry'. The second approach is to look at it from the other side, and ask 'What is the point in not living?' Usually, one would reply that one has nothing to gain and no more to lose by not doing so. Neither approach is altogether satisfactory. The first reduces

one's life to the sum of the thoughts and acts of a single mind and body, because it's just describing the activity of living. The second can't satisfy those who genuinely think their continued existence is too painful for all concerned to justify it. Both approaches fail because any description of a life 'from the outside' fails to capture what is most essential about it, that it is our life. Each person is left, therefore, to specify a point (or end) to their own living for themselves. It can be given to you, but only in so far as you are willing to take it on board as entirely your own. Sorry I can't be more helpful. Try drugs, and you can forget the problem; or religion, and get a made-to-measure answer.
Charles Cohen, Wadham College, Oxford.

□ THIS is easy. I understand (not being an Anglican myself) that the Church of England catechism says: 'Man's chief end is to glorify God and to enjoy Him for ever.'
Heather Lloyd, Glasgow.

□ THE philosopher's answer:
1. 'To be is to do' (Socrates); 'To do is to be' (Sartre); 'Do be do be do' (Frank Sinatra).
2. According to Nietzsche, or I should say the wise Satyr Silenus, quoted by Nietzsche in *The Birth of Tragedy from the Spirit of Music*, there is no point to living. When hunted down and caught by King Midas, the wise Satyr Silenus, companion to Dionysus, answers Midas's question on what is the ultimate truth. 'Not to have been born, to be nothing,' he replies. 'But the second best is to die soon!' There you have it, right from the Satyr's mouth.
3. On the other hand, Albert Camus, in *The Myth of Sisyphus*, came to the conclusion that even in lives of little hope and extreme adversity, there are moments or sus- pended lulls in the tension when one can relax and view the world around one and one's meaning in relation to the world. Thus, Sisyphus, forced for eternity to push a boulder up to the top of a mountain only for it to roll back down the

mountain again, could at least relax and recharge his batteries, and recognise his essential oneness with nature and the world around him in those moments when he had to walk back down the mountain to retrieve his boulder. By being at least conscious of the absurdity of his life, Sisyphus is happy. His consciousness ties him to the wholeness of nature and also to his essential freedom, which means that he cannot be dominated either by nature or by the gods who force him to push the boulder up the mountain: 'There is no fate that cannot be surmounted by scorn,' Camus says.
Nigel Polkinghorne, Penzance, Cornwall.

☐ THE point of anything is what comes at the end of it. The end of life is death — so death is the point of living.
(Dr) William Johnston, Arnside, Cumbria.

QUESTION: Given the availability of all known building materials and ideal rock to build on, what would be the height of the highest building that could be built today? What would be the constraining factor?

☐ WITH an infinite budget the normal limits of high-rise construction are removed. Loading can safely be distributed into the world's strongest bedrock using massive foundations. Overall stability against wind loading and buckling will be assured if the building is allowed enough ground to be self-bracing. So, in pure structural terms, the controlling factor is the ability of the building frame to carry vertical loading. Assuming the building is a residential block (office loading is greater) and using solid steel columns of sensible style and spacing, to allow the building to be properly inhabited, an overall height of about 1,250 metres (450 storeys) is possible. A steel 'Eiffel' tower about 4,000 metres high is possible. I hope you realise that we are five years too late to get funding for this type of development.
Ian Hunt, London N10.

☐ IF WE define buildings as man-made edifices above ground and containing spaces allowing humans to move about within the structure, then the pyramids of Egypt and Central America are buildings. Mount Everest is a natural pyramid; therefore, using granite blocks a conical or pyramidal building could be erected to a height of at least 10,000 metres. The actual constraining factors would be geological. Isostatic downwarping of the crust beneath the enormous weight of the structure would cause faults in the rock mass, while metamorphic processes at the core of the pyramid (melting of certain minerals in the granite due to pressure) would result in instability and collapse. These constraints could be overcome by giving the building a honeycomb or lattice structure and using a variety of lighter and more tensile materials than granite. Living spaces within the cone/pyramid could be provided, so creating a city perhaps tens of thousands of metres high. There would be increasing problems in supplying the higher levels with water, fuel, waste disposal and so forth and there would be complex ecological and climatic challenges to the architects. But perhaps the ultimate constraining factor is human nature: the general unpopularity of high-rise flats and the biblical myth of the Tower of Babel suggest why such a conical mega-city could not succeed.
Michael Ghirelli, Hillesden, Bucks.

QUESTION: Last summer, I and three friends went camping in France. The mosquitoes feasted upon two of us but barely touched the other two. How do they know who the succulent ones are?

☐ I HAVE a theory that most bloodthirsty insects are not attracted to people with O-negative blood. I have this type of blood and am very rarely, if ever, bitten. This theory also applies to my husband. Friends who are O-negative have

also found themselves to be the only ones unbitten, while others suffer badly.
Valerie Stevens, Burnham-on-Sea, Somerset.

☐ AS SOMEONE with O-negative blood who gets eaten alive by mosquitoes, I disagree with Valerie Stevens. I do, however, have an oily complexion while an O-positive friend who has never been bitten by a mosquito has a very dry skin.
(Mrs) May Robertson, East Kilbride, Glasgow.

☐ I AM told that the way to counteract mosquito bites is to consume garlic. Consumption of the garlic should begin some time before exposure to the insects, but I do not know whether the garlic actually prevents the bites occurring or merely prevents the irritating reaction to the bites. However, it does appear to work.
M. F. Wall, Perton, nr Wolverhampton.

☐ MOSQUITOES can distinguish contrasting shades of clothing, though the actual colour doesn't matter. If you have a dark complexion, wear dark clothes; if you're pale, dress in white. Wearing black trousers with a white shirt is as good as inviting a mosquito over for dinner. But while your clothes may catch a mosquito's attention, it will only sting you if you smell right. We all emit our own peculiar body odour, which is based on a number of factors, most of which we have no control over. The food we eat is about the only contributing factor we can control. There are all kinds of crazy myths about what you should eat to repel mosquitoes. Gold prospectors in the Canadian Arctic in the 1940s claimed that eating bananas kept the mosquitoes away. In a more scientific vein, evidence has shown that mosquitoes are less attracted to people with a high count of Vitamin B. Beer has lots of Vitamin B, so you could try drinking that on your summer holiday and if it doesn't work . . . well, if you drink enough of it you won't notice the mosquitoes much anyway.
Doug Holmes, London SW14.

☐ I USED to be bitten by mosquitoes until I was put permanently on steroids after an operation a few years ago, since when they have never touched me. Unfortunately for most people, steroids are far too strong a drug to be used merely as an insect repellant, but I wonder if other medication can have the same effect.
Tim Gooderham, London W1.

☐ WHEN I lived in the tropics the mosquitoes avoided me when I was pregnant.
Caroline Sassoon, Fowey, Cornwall.

QUESTION: Why, when the telephone handpiece is picked up and put down without rotating, does the curly flex gradually coil up more and more?

☐ PEOPLE tend to pick up a phone with their favoured hand. When this hand is then needed, for instance to write a message, the phone will be transferred to the other hand (and the other ear). If the phone is then replaced with this hand, a twist will have been introduced. I suspect that the problem is rare in households where the phone is used equally by left- and right-handed people.
Paul Holister, Amsterdam, Netherlands.

QUESTION: If you can have cows' milk, goats' milk and sheep's milk, both to drink and in a variety of cheeses, why not pigs' milk?

☐ PIGS are much more difficult to milk. In cows, sheep and goats the milk is available more or less on tap and 'let-down' of the milk is easily stimulated, even by a milking machine. Pigs, however, are much more fussy as to when they make milk available. Whereas cattle and sheep only tend to have one or two offspring at a time, a sow may have

between eight and 14 in a litter. If milk was freely available it would be difficult to keep track of who had been fed. To get round this problem, a sow will only 'let down' milk when all the litter is suckling at the same time. Therefore, to milk a sow it would be necessary to simulate a large number of suckling piglets. Even real piglets don't find it easy to get milk and often need to undertake around 2–3 minutes of synchronised sucking before any milk is released, and then it is only for a few seconds.
Duncan Law, London N7.

QUESTION: What danger will result from not completing a course of prescribed antibiotics?

☐ THE danger to the individual is that the infection will recur, and will be more difficult to treat when it does. The danger to the rest of us is that the general population of the infecting bacterium will become more resistant to the antibiotic concerned. If you fail to complete a course of antibiotics, some of the bacteria causing the infection may survive – and these will be the ones with the greatest resistance to the antibiotic. This is an unnatural version of natural selection, and will result in the bacterial population in the afflicted patient having a higher than normal resistance to that antibiotic. As the surviving bacteria reproduce, the resulting infection would not be treatable with the same antibiotic. If the infection is passed on to someone else, their infection will also be resistant to the antibiotic.
Jim Lodge, London SE4.

☐ WITH due respect to Jim Lodge, his reply is somewhat ambiguous. Who decides what a 'course' of antibiotics should be? The patient consults the doctor who decides that the patient suffers from a bacterial infection. A course of antibiotics is prescribed and the patient recovers. Was this happy event due to the antibiotic? If, on the other hand, the patient does not recover, the doctor may send the patient's specimens to the local laboratory who will then, hopefully, advise the doctor as to which antibiotic will be most effective. Has the first antibiotic resulted in resistant bacteria since it was obviously inadequate? Would an effective antibiotic kill the offending bacteria almost immediately, say within 48 hours? If the drug manufacturers know the antibiotic is effective in 48 hours then a recommended five-day treatment would keep everybody happy, including their shareholders.

Allan Wilson, Pharmacist, Comrie, Perthshire.

☐ AS A pharmacist, Allan Wilson should know better if he is suggesting that antibiotic courses are too long. A number of factors will determine how long it takes even an effective antibiotic to eliminate an infection. These include the fact that there are areas of the body where antibiotics do not achieve good penetration (e.g. the lungs and sinuses). The quantity of infective material that may have built up in the body, and from which re-infection may occur, must also be taken into account. Lastly, the extent to which the body's own immune activity has to be responsible for the final elimination of an infective agent must be considered. Allan Wilson is right about one thing, though. If you are taking an antibiotic and can perceive no impact on the infection within 48 hours, you should return to your doctor and request a culture or further investigation.

Alan Scott, Lewes, E. Sussex.

☐ WHAT about the danger arising from taking more than one may need? I understand that antibiotics act rather like the SAS: in knocking out the enemy bacteria, they also do damage to one's own immune system. Can anyone elaborate with authority on this? I understand that the broad-spectrum antibiotics are the worst offenders in this respect. After taking two courses of antibiotics, I have suddenly

developed a range of minor ailments, including catarrh, eye irritations, foot infection, etc., which I have never suffered before.
Mary Ingham, Ramsgate, Kent.

QUESTION: It is commonly believed that a screw propeller for ships is more efficient than a paddle wheel. Have there been any experiments under properly controlled conditions?

☐ THE event that settled the argument took place in April 1845. The screw-driven *Rattler* and the paddle steamer *Necto*, both ships of similar size and power, were joined stern to stern and engaged in a bizarre tug-o'-war in the North Sea. The winner was the 200 hp *Rattler*, which towed the *Necto* backwards for 5 miles at 2½ knots.
Julian Frost, Leighton Buzzard, Beds.

☐ FOR long-distance journeys ships driven by screw propellers have a number of advantages over their paddle wheel counterparts. For example screw propellers, unlike paddle wheels, are in constant contact with the water. During rough weather ships rock from side to side – which means that paddle wheels periodically rise out of the water, causing a reduction in efficiency. Furthermore, as fuel is burned to power the engines, ships become lighter and rise out of the water. This again reduces the contact between paddle wheel and water and hence overall efficiency.
Edward Duffy, Stockport, Cheshire.

QUESTION: I think the longest English word you can touch type with one hand is 'afterwards'. Can anyone better this?

☐ REVERBERATED.
Gaynelle Samuel, London E8.

☐ EXTRAVASATED. If you really want to practise with one hand, try: 'Extra vegetated terraces were reseeded afterwards as we recreated a devastated desert. We faced a savage crew, sewed seaweed sweaters, as we extracted stewed sewage.'
Alastair Milne, Den Haag, Netherlands.

☐ THE longest word you can type with your right hand is 'monopoly'. Why not try to find the longest coherent sentence for each hand, e.g. 'I jump on my polo pony'? It beats working.
Elisabeth Manning, Droitwich, Worcs.

☐ DESEGREGATED watercresses are longer one-handed words. Further examples are in my left-handed lament to Labour's latest loss. Had it not involved a compromise with my right hand, I'd have called it 'Left Out, or the Sound of One Hand Tapping'. The last word of the poem, a 14-letter description of John Major's majority, should close off further correspondence about the longest word you can touch type with one hand: it could go on for ever . . .

Defeat

A reverse we reasserted
afterwards
Stewardesses axed taxes
Effects are exaggerated we
asseverated
VAT reaggregated are C2s
devastated
We readdressed refettered greed
We were defeated Redefeated
Reredefeated
Desecrated redevastated
A decade 2 far we reasseverated
Aftereffects are a Q 4 1
2 zzzzzzzzzzzzz

Paul Fisher, Bath

QUESTION: Can white people become Rastafarians?

☐ AS RASTAFARIANISM has no official dogma and no formal 'church', there is no conversion process. The nearest thing to a church that Rastas have is the Twelve Tribes of Israel Church, which is multi-racial and will accept anyone, without a ceremony, who recognises Haile Selassie I to be one of a long line of prophets. Although it is possible to be a 'clean-face, baldhead' Rasta, most Rastafarians follow the Nazarites in that they do not use combs or razors (hence beard and dreadlocks) and do not practise any sort of body piercing or tattooing. Also, most Rastafarians follow some or all of the Pentateuchal dietary laws and live lives not dissimilar to Orthodox Jews. The use of marijuana is not as widespread as the media would like us to believe and alcohol is almost invariably not taken. Belief in H. I. M. Haile Selassie as God Himself has taken a blow recently as the Lion of Judah's body has been found. Many Rastas will choose not to believe this, as God can never die and 'Jah live'. Many see Ras Tafari as the final prophet following Jesus, Mohammed, etc., before the fall of Babylon. This illustrates the wide range of belief among Rastas. Therefore, to become a Rasta, one must believe Haile Selassie to be at least a prophet descended from Solomon, practise a pious lifestyle and be righteous, but most importantly gain acceptance among a group of believing Rastafarians. This is not as difficult as it seems for a white person. To find out how to live as a Rasta, just ask one of us.
Ras Mikey Simeon, Manchester.

QUESTION: On a piano, harpsichord or organ keyboard, the white keys represent the key of C. Why not the key of A?

☐ THEY do represent the key of A — A minor. It may be that this key was originally given the 'A' status because of its serious nature, compared to the more frivolous major, and it is interesting to note that, on many early instruments, these keys are black, not white. Why, however, in this case, did they call it 'minor'? A good question which my mind, currently whirling with the enigma of Majors conjuring majorities out of minorities, is far too confused to contemplate, let alone answer.

A. E. Baker, Kettering, Northants.

☐ THE white notes of a keyboard obviously don't represent the 'key' of C until they are used in a context which indicates that the music is 'in' C major. What they do represent, in their arrangement of tones and semitones, is the diatonic major scale (or mode) of C. So really the question is: why is the natural mode of the keyboard not named after the first letter of the alphabet? The white notes include many other possible scale formations: not only the minor, with A as tonic (the old Aeolian mode), but the Dorian mode (tonic D), the Phrygian (tonic E), the Lydian (tonic F) and so on, each made up of a different sequence of tones and semitones. The first instrument to be provided with a keyboard, the organ, originally had only 'white' keys and was used to play melodies in the various modes, the lowest note in use at the time being designated A. The G below was later added under the name 'gamma ut' (hence the word 'gamut'), and the 'black' keys were added one at a time, starting with B flat, for the purposes of transposition. In a sense it is a historical accident that the name C was applied to the keynote of the mode (Ionian) which, as the 'major scale', later became predominant in Western music. I should point out that on the Continent, notes are named after syllables of a Latin hymn whose successive phrases began on successive degrees of the scale: ut, re, mi, fa, etc. Ut, which originally could signify C, F or G, has become fixed as C. So in France the major scale playable on the keyboard without the use of sharps or flats is the first in the system of nomenclature.

Thelma Grimsdyke, Cheltenham, Glos.

QUESTION: I was once told that it is possible to drill a perfectly square hole using a rotating bit. I still don't believe it. Can it be done?

□ A SQUARE hole can indeed be drilled but the process is not simple. One has to clamp a square template over the desired hole. The drill bit has three cutting blades. It also has an eccentric drive so that its centre is not fixed; in this way its cutting edges can follow the sides of the square template. The idea is described in H. J. Watts's US Patents 1,241,175–7 of 25 September 1917. This is an application of the famous Reuleaux triangle – a non-circular curve of constant width, like the current 20p and 50p coins. The Reuleaux triangle is also the basis of the Wankel rotating piston engine.
David Singmaster, South Bank Polytechnic, London SE1.

□ CABINET-makers routinely perform this apparent miracle with the aid of a hollow-chisel morticer. The machine plunges a square-sectioned hollow chisel, containing a rotating auger bit, into the wood; the auger removes the majority of the waste, while the chisel pares out the corners of the square hole.
Roger Cash, Cabinet-Maker, Eynsham, Oxon.

QUESTION: When and why did bunny-rabbits get involved with Easter?

□ RABBITS' involvement derives from the transfer of folklore originally attributable to the hare. Hares are indigenous to Britain and were sacred animals in pre-Christian times, whereas the rabbit was introduced into this country by the Normans. Both are prolific reproducers and thus are associated with the birth and renewal of springtime, the season in which Easter falls. (The Christian rebirth narrative of the Resurrection was superimposed on to the pagan Saxon

festival of spring and renewal, dedicated to the goddess
Eostre, or Easter.) It was taboo to eat hare-meat in Celtic
times and it is said that Boudicca (Boadicea) took a hare into
battle with her. Hares and rabbits were both associated with
luck, giving rise to the rabbit's-foot charms. It was also
thought that witches could turn themselves into hares and in
such form could only be killed with a silver bullet. Eggs, too,
have 'new birth' connotations, and in Europe the hare is
traditionally the bringer of Easter eggs.
Eric Fitch, Burnham, Bucks.

□ IT WAS probably St Bede of Jarrow (673–735) who
converted the pagan festival of Eostre into the Christian
festival celebrating Christ's Resurrection. However, old customs die hard and local traditions associated with the
worship of the pagan goddess, during which hares were
almost certainly sacrificed, may have survived. For example,
on Easter Monday in Hallaton in Leicestershire there is the
Hare Pie Scramble, in which pieces of the pie are thrown to
the crowd which gathers on a mound known as Hare Pie
Bank, just outside the village. It is said that this custom goes
back several centuries to a local woman who had been saved
from being gored to death by a bull when a hare ran across
its path, causing it to hesitate. In gratitude she gave land to
the church on condition that two hare pies should be distributed to the parishioners every year. It is interesting that the
words for 'Easter' in most other European languages derive
from Pesach, the Hebrew name for the Passover festival (e.g.
Pâques in French, Pasqua in Italian and Pask in Swedish). It
was this festival which was being celebrated by Jews at the
time of Jesus's crucifixion.
Linda Holmes, Cottingham, N. Humberside.

**QUESTION: Why are Catholics sometimes called
'left-footers'?**

□ THE answer lies in the rich folklore of the humble spade — and provides a good illustration of the inadequacy of calling a spade 'a spade'. The saying turns on a traditional distinction between left- and right-handed spades in Irish agriculture. It has been used as a figure of speech and often, sadly, as a term of abuse to distinguish Protestants from Catholics: 'He digs with the wrong foot.' Most types of digging spade in Britain and Ireland have foot-rests at the top of their blades; two-sided spades have foot-rests on each side of the shaft and socket, while an older style of one-sided spade had only one. Two-sided spades may well have been introduced by the Protestant 'planters' in the sixteenth century. By the early nineteenth century specialised spade and shovel mills in the north of Ireland were producing vast numbers of two-sided spades which came to be universally used in Ulster and strongly identified with the province. One-sided spades with narrow blades and a foot-rest cut out of the side of the relatively larger wooden shaft continued in use in the south and west. The rural population of Gaelic Ireland retained the Catholic faith and tended also to retain the one-sided spade and 'dig with the wrong foot'. In fact, the two-sided spade of Ulster was generally used with the left foot whereas the one-sided spade tended to be used with the right foot. Instinctively, the 'wrong foot' of the Catholics has come to be thought of as the left foot. The figure of speech has now been extended to kicking with the wrong foot.

Hugh Cheape, National Museums of Scotland, Edinburgh.

QUESTION: What is the best type of wax to wax a moustache with? Where can one get it? Is there a special technique for applying it?

□ THE best type of wax to use is, surprisingly, moustache wax. Geo. F. Trumper of Curzon Street in London stock what appears to be the only available brand, manufactured

by Ed Pinaud Inc. of New York. Its main ingredient is beeswax and it comes in five colours. It should be used sparingly, particularly in the case of the brown and black shades: one smudge on a finger can decorate a room, H-block style. A note of caution. When I first waxed my moustache many years ago I expected some negative attention on appearing in public and I was not disappointed. I was caught in a sudden downpour but remained resolute in the knowledge that my moustache, encased in (coloured) wax, would resist the effects of the rain, since wax resists water. I bore the laughter and the stares until I reached my studio. There, in the mirror, the awful truth was revealed. The moustache wax had dissolved in the rain (it is water soluble – how else would one wash it off?), leaving two brown streaks running down each side of my face and on to my crisp, white, starched collar.
Christopher Sharrock, Brighton, E. Sussex.

□ A THICK, clear hairdressing wax, such as Black and White, manufactured by Windsor Laboratories of Jamaica, has proved, in my experience, eminently suitable. It is available from the more street-wise hairdressers, especially those catering for Afro-Caribbean tastes. Aided only by a mirror, it is possible to achieve structurally sound horizontal spans in excess of 160 mm.
Jurek Blaszczak, Harrow, Middx.

□ OBVIOUSLY none of your other readers has been to see the film *Hook*. Captain Hook (Dustin Hoffman) has a moustache which he wants his mate, Smee (Bob Hoskins), to groom. Smee performs the task by poking his fingers in his ears and then grooming Hook's moustache with this home-grown wax. An admirable solution for *Guardian* readers who wish to be organic and recycling (and revolting).
Brian Westbury, Loughton, Essex.

QUESTION: When, where and who was the first 'spin doctor'? Who coined the term?

□ 'SPIN doctor' developed in the jargon of US politics. It is a senior political spokesperson employed to promote a favourable interpretation of events to journalists. The phrase was first used in print in October 1984 in an editorial in the *New York Times* about the aftermath of the televised debate between US presidential candidates Ronald Reagan and Walter Mondale. Donald Regan, former White House chief of staff, was informally known as the Director of Spin Control. The term 'spin doctor' is formed by compounding. In US politics 'spin' is interpretation, the bias or slant put on information when it is presented to the public or in a press conference; all information can have positive or negative 'spin'. This is a sporting metaphor (for example, spin put on a ball in cricket or baseball). 'Doctor' comes from the various figurative uses of the verb 'to doctor', ranging from 'patch up' or 'mend' to 'falsify'.
Nicholas E. Gough, Malmesbury, Wilts.

QUESTION: Do intellectuals serve any useful purpose? If so, what?

□ ONE purpose they serve is that of asking whether things are valuable only insofar as they are useful. Would an answer to the question be useful?
R.W. Davies, Department of Philosophy, University of Birmingham.

□ YES. Read Arthur Koestler's essay 'The Intelligentsia'.
Peter Young, Crawley, W. Sussex.

QUESTION: Has anyone ever constructed a study to determine whether animals or birds refer to each other

by name? It seems reasonable to suppose that they, no less than ourselves, need to be able to get one another's attention on an individual, as opposed to a merely undifferentiated, basis.

☐ THERE are only a few species that exist in sufficiently close-knit groups to merit recognition of individuals. In a typical social interaction the pecking order of a bird-table, for example ritualised displays of dominance and subordination occur, obviating the need for individual recognition *per se*. Individual recognition would be necessary only in highly structured social groups where reciprocal altruism takes place. Olive baboons which have been aided in fights by other members of the troop, tend to return the favour. This requires recognition (presumably visual), but a familiar face does not need a name attached, even in human circles. Other 'model social groups' include the bees. Certain species demonstrate a finely tuned level of recognition whereby members will welcome close relatives into the nest more readily than distant kin. Smell seems to be the agent of recognition in this case.
Bob Sambrook, Southampton.

QUESTION: On a visit to Formentera in the Balearic Islands, I saw a monument to Jules Verne. I was told that he spent some time there and that the island figured in one of his novels. Can anyone throw light on this?

☐ THE story is *Hector Servadac, or The Career of a Comet*, in which the hero visits Formentera by travelling on a wind-powered sledge, in the hope of finding the mysterious and irascible Professor Palmyrin Rosette who may explain why the Mediterranean is frozen and a chunk of Algeria is pursuing an elliptical trajectory around the Sun. An English edition was published by Sampson Low, Marston, Searle &

Rivington in 1878 with 98 jolly illustrations which are
rather more convincing than the narrative.
G. J. K. Griffin, Stamford, Lincs.

QUESTION: How can I become a lighthouse keeper?

☐ TRINITY House, the General Lighthouse Authority for
England, Wales and the Channel Islands, ceased recruiting
lighthouse keepers in 1980 because of automation. For the
record, applicants had to be aged 19–32 and were required
to pass an IQ test and strict medical examinations.
H. L. Cooper, Trinity House, London EC3.

**QUESTION: During a recent spell of hot weather I was
assured by a colleague that I would cool more quickly if
I drank steaming hot tea rather than a cold drink. I find
this hard to believe but who is right?**

☐ THE body's temperature control mechanism, known as
homoeostasis, will equalise the temperature between the
body's core and its periphery. By increasing one's body
temperature, e.g. by drinking hot tea, the body's homoeos-
tatic mechanism will cool down its peripheral temperature.
Therefore hot tea on a hot day will make you feel cooler than
a cold drink.
David Lypnyj, Acton, London W3.

☐ MR LYPNYJ'S physiology is unconvincing. The body will
respond to a rise in central core temperature by giving up
heat from the periphery by increasing skin blood flow (and if
necessary by sweat). Increased skin blood flow makes one
feel warm, not cool. The difference between hot tea and a
cold drink may be marginal but we have yet to see Boris
Becker asking for hot tea between sets.
(Dr) D. W. Barritt, Long Ashton, Bristol.

QUESTION: One can buy magnetic water softeners which clip on to the outside of the cold water supply. Do they work, and if so how?

☐ WATER conditioners do not soften water. They zap it with powerful magnets, 'causing the hard ions to remain in suspension and not be deposited as scale'. In 1985, *Which?* magazine tested several types of magnetic water conditioners and found none of them to have any effect in reducing the scale deposited by hard water. I summarised the *Which?* results in a trade magazine and was subsequently contacted by a manufacturer whose conditioner had not been included in the *Which?* tests. He offered me one on permanent loan for evaluation. I have evaluated it for six years. I can confirm that it was quickly and easily installed, that its running costs are zero and that it looks very impressive. But effective it ain't. I could achieve as much scale reduction by banging on the side of the cold water tank and demanding that the ions come out with their hands up.
Anthony Mundy, London E4.

QUESTION: Is it possible to obtain a radio set capable of picking up the sound of the TV channels?

☐ IN THE US you can buy cheapish radios which also pick up TV sound but in the UK your best bet is to buy a scanner. The coverage you need is from 477.25 MHz (Channel 21) to 861.25 MHz (Channel 69). Sound channels occur every 8 MHz, so Channel 22 is 485.25 MHz, Channel 23 is 493.25 MHz and so on. The scanner needs to be capable of receiving wide-band FM, as the usual FM on scanners is for the reception of walkie-talkie type transmissions. This sort of equipment in a portable format will cost around £250. American 'TV sound' radios are useless in the UK.
Hugo Cornwall, London N4.

☐ A TV Nicam tuner– decoder, bought from a specialist hi-fi dealer, can be tuned to the four TV channels. It can be connected to a stereo amplifier and twin speakers to give excellent quality sound – far better than the average Nicam TV set. The sound can be in mono or stereo, depending on whether the TV channel has stereo facilities and whether the programme was made with stereo sound.
N. F. Farrands, Wolverhampton.

☐ THERE is a TV sound-only receiver available through RNIB Customer Services, PO Box 173, Peterborough, PE2 0WS (tel. 0345 023153). This is available to all registered blind people at £59 and to others at £112.
P. Dickinson, Rehabilitation Officer for the Visually Impaired, Leeds.

QUESTION: The daily allowance of a twelfth-century English Chancellor included one wax candle and '40 candle ends'. Does it mean that the stubs of partly burnt candles were collected for recycling?

☐ THESE would have been beeswax candles which were always comparatively expensive, and the unburnt portions would have been valuable perquisites. My own history of *The Waxchandlers of London* (Phillimore, 1973) gives examples of the penalties for adulteration or dealing in 'naughty wax'. I have some partly burnt candles collected from the choir stalls by an ancestor following the funeral of William IV in Westminster Abbey.
John Dummelow, Lincoln.

☐ IN THE winter of 1977–8, when power cuts occurred in London, each civil servant in the offices where I worked was issued with one candle. I shared a room with one other official, hence two candles. Weeks later the messengers came round to collect the candle ends; my fellow worker had by

then left (with his candle) and I was cross-questioned as to why I could produce only one. The candle-end mentality of Chancellors, or at least treasury officials, must have been remarkably enduring.
Chris Sladen, London W5.

QUESTION: What happens to a dead person's premium bond? (A recent storyline in *The Archers* suggested that descendants of the deceased couldn't claim the prize if the number came up.)

□ UNLESS a bond is repaid in the meantime, it can go on winning prizes for a full year after the end of the month in which the holder died. Any prizes won during this time go to the estate. In the *Archers* storyline, Joe Grundy is notified of a prize drawn in the name of his wife who had died several years earlier. Characteristically he had failed to notify the Premium Bond Office of her death, so her bonds were still taking part in prize draws. Joe is not entitled to the prize but tries to claim the prize money (illegally). Eventually the prize is returned to the Premium Bond Office after Joe's bank refuses to allow him to negotiate the warrant. In real life a prize like this would be reallocated to the next eligible bond number.
Alan McGill, Controller, National Savings, Lytham, Lancs.

QUESTION: Who was the man who struck the gong for J. Arthur Rank?

□ I HAVE never had it verified but, as a young lad, I always understood from an elderly relative that J. Arthur's gong bonger was Jerome K. Jerome, the author of *Three Men in a Boat*. I have a sneaking feeling that this may not be true; perhaps someone can put my mind at rest.
Michael Manning, Chessington, Surrey.

☐ THE trademark of a musclebound man banging a gong at the beginning of every Rank film was dreamed up in the 1930s by the publicity manageress of General Film Distributors, which then distributed J. Arthur's films. The lady had in mind Bombadier Billy Wells, 'Beautiful Billy' to his fans, who had been British heavyweight boxing champion from 1911 to 1919. He was filmed at Walton Hall Studios, Isleworth, in 1935. After the war, it was deemed that Wells should be replaced and his successor was hunky Phil Nieman, who was immortalised at Gainsborough Studios, Shepherd's Bush. Nieman's replacement, in 1955, was yet another athlete, Ken Richmond, who won a wrestling bronze in the 1952 Helsinki Olympics. Richmond, filmed at Pinewood, remains to this day. Incidentally, the gong is actually made of plaster and paper and the noise we hear, the reverberations of a Chinese tam-tam (three feet diameter), is recorded by percussionist James Blades.
Quentin Falk, Little Marlow, Bucks.

QUESTION: Where can I get an Ecu?

☐ ECU coins have been minted by France, Belgium, Spain and Ireland. All are commemorative and only of interest to collectors. However, Gibraltar has now minted a gold coin with a face value of 70 Ecu (£50 sterling), with the Queen's head on one side, designed for circulation.
Michael Downs, London EC2.

☐ WE took Ecu travellers' cheques to France this summer. The bank in Salon, Provence, could not find the exchange rate on its computer, and it took some time to negotiate an exchange of currency!
Joanna Fulford, Pateley Bridge, N. Yorks.

QUESTION: Why German measles? Why not French or English?

☐ IT IS a corruption of 'germane', meaning 'like or akin to' measles.
Dr (signature illegible), Blandford, Dorset.

QUESTION: Who were Buck of Buck's Fizz and Pimm of Pimm's No. 1, and what were the original ingredients?

☐ CHAMPAGNE lovers may know the origin of Buck's Fizz, but I can certainly tell you how Pimm's No. 1 came about. This unusual drink, quintessentially associated with the English summer, was invented in 1840 by a certain James Pimm, the owner of an oyster bar which stood in Poultry in the City of London. As word of Pimm's unique creation spread, customers began flocking to Pimm's Oyster Bar to sample it and, soon after, gentlemen's clubs in the West End were ordering supplies of Pimm's 'cup' – a reference to the tankards from which it was drunk. However, it was not until 1859, by which time his original Poultry establishment had grown into a sizeable chain, that Pimm began bottling his drink. The way was now open for sales throughout Britain and the Empire. The first Pimm's Cup was based on gin, but gradually new types were introduced. Pimm's No. 1 is the original gin-based drink, but at the height of its popularity Pimm's boasted six different varieties, including Scotch (No. 2) and vodka (No. 6). The recipe is still a closely guarded secret. All its manufacturers will say is that it is a blend of liqueurs, herbs and spices with a base of gin.
John Davies, London N10.

QUESTION: If one wishes to prospect for gold in rivers in England and Wales, whose permission must be sought?

☐ THE permission of the riparian owners on both banks and

the fishery owner is required. In addition, a legal right of access to the river is needed. More importantly, the act of panning must not cause pollution nor harm fish, the spawn of fish or the food of fish (Salmon & Freshwater Fisheries Act 1975 and Water Resources Act 1991).
A. G. Dixon, Divisional Scientist, National Rivers Authority, Welsh Region, Caernarfon, Gwynedd.

QUESTION: In *My Country Right or Wrong*, George Orwell writes of the London evening newspapers: 'I remember the pile of peagreen papers . . .' Why green? When did they change and why?

☐ THE one and only green London evening newspaper was the *Westminster Gazette*, launched by George Newnes on a no doubt surprised public on 31 January 1893. On sea-green rather than pea-green newsprint, the novelty was introduced thus: 'Evening papers are largely read by people going home in badly lighted railway carriages, omnibuses etc. White paper and black ink may do very well for a reader sitting at home on a steady floor and with sufficient light; but to try and read by the gloomy thing in the roof which railway companies are pleased to call a light while jolted about in a railway carriage is very injurious to the eyesight.' The *Westminster Gazette* stuck by its green principles and practice until it was switched to morning publication in 1921. It is interesting to record that the *Gazette* made its bow less than a month after the *Financial Times* turned to '*FT* peach' – maintained of course to this day.
David Linton, Hon. Librarian, London Press Club.

☐ ONE green paper is alive and well in Sheffield. The Saturday sports edition of the *Sheffield Star* is printed on green paper and known to us all as the Green 'Un.
Simon Turney, Sheffield.

QUESTION: If the three wise men from the east followed a star to their east (Matthew, chapter 2) how did they reach Bethlehem? They would have needed to follow a star to their west, surely.

☐ CORRECT. The Magi did follow a star in a westerly direction, but let us not forget that they were, after all, wise men, and therefore probably not given to hasty actions. The Greek word *anatole* used by Matthew implies 'the direction of rising', so in rendering this as 'east' it should be understood as a general direction rather than a precise heading. It is not too fanciful to infer that they made further observations and deliberations over a lengthy period before concluding that the star (or whatever) was so portentous as to warrant following. By this time the object could well have been setting in the west, the direction in which the Magi eventually travelled.
Alan Linfield, Tring, Herts.

☐ IT IS a basic misunderstanding of navigation to imagine that one actually 'follows' a star. Imagine you are walking on the moors and can see a single tree some miles off. By walking towards it, you will remain on a constant compass bearing and eventually reach it. On the other hand, if you knew you wanted to head east, you could navigate by walking away from the tree, keeping it on a constant bearing on your compass. With the tree (or indeed a star) you follow a bearing rather than the object. Anyone can use a star to steer by. If you know you want to go north, just keep the pole star (Polaris, which happens to be almost exactly above the north pole) ahead of you. If you want to go south, keep it on your back. East and you must keep it on your left shoulder. This is not very accurate, but for short distances it might be good enough. Proper celestial navigation is more complicated, because all heavenly objects are in motion relative to an earthbound observer. The stars will appear to whirl round the sky because the earth spins daily on its axis. They

change their apparent position with the seasons, as the earth tilts on its axis. They will seem to alter position according to the observer's latitude. The calculations required to compensate for their motions are very tricky. You will need a very accurate watch, a sextant, an almanac, a magnetic compass, a view of the horizon at sea level and knowledge of the equations to work it all out. The three wise men had none of these.
Marcus Palliser, London W14.

QUESTION: What is the origin of the peculiar habit of the clergy of wearing a dog collar?

☐ A DOG collar is a reversed God collar.
Robin Boyes, Scarborough, N. Yorks.

☐ IT GOES back to the arrival in this country of Father Gentili, of the Roman Catholic order of the Institute of Charity. He came in the 1840s to preach a mission and the habit of his order incorporated a circular collar of the kind now familiar to us. At that time, clergy of all denominations usually wore a white stock but Father Gentili's collar created a vogue, at first among his fellow Catholic priests and later among all clergy. By the end of the century it was in common use. The term 'dog collar' is frequently resented by clerics; it was at first called a 'Roman collar'.
Tony Glynn, Manchester 14.

QUESTION: There is a story that when the mob stormed the Bastille in 1789 they released an Englishman who had been held there for more than 20 years. Who was he and what became of him?

☐ ACCORDING to Simon Schama's book *Citizens* (Penguin, 1989), a 'Major White' – described by the French as English

and by the English as Irish – was incarcerated in the Bastille as a lunatic at the time of its storming. He was released and paraded round the streets by the mob. He continued to believe that he was Julius Caesar and was later sent to Charenton Asylum (also home to the Marquis de Sade at that time).
Beverlie Drewitt, Redditch, Worcs.

QUESTION: I bought a pair of love spoons while on holiday in the Lake District. They are intricately carved. What is their origin?

☐ AS A Welshman, I have always believed the love spoon to be an exclusively Welsh folk craft. They were made by young men to be given to young women as a token of affection. The effort involved in carving was a measure of the man's devotion, serving to cement an already extant relationship or to express a desire to start one. The symbols used all had a meaning – for example, a chain indicated a strong bond. If my memory serves me correctly, the number of balls trapped between four rails in one of the most common designs indicated the number of children hoped for from a future marriage. I am surprised to hear of them being found in the Lake District. Perhaps there is a connection with Wales in the historical link that (along with Cornwall and Strathclyde) these areas were peopled with original Britons long after the Saxons took over the rest of Britain. I suspect it is more likely to be in their shared status as tourist areas with the concomitant need to offer 'traditional' souvenirs.
N. J. Morgan, Thurso, Caithness.

☐ THE carving of a wooden love spoon was the traditional way of ensuring that Welsh lovers kept their hands to themselves.
Judith Morgan, Doncaster.

QUESTION: A character in a Raymond Chandler novel described some furniture as 'looking as though it had been bought in a borax emporium'. What is a borax emporium?

☐ PHILIP Marlowe himself uses the term in *The High Window* to describe furnishings 'on which a great deal of expense had been spared'. *Webster's Ninth New Collegiate Dictionary* gives the first recorded use as 1932, probably from Yiddish, and meaning cheap, shoddy merchandise. Leo Rosten, in *The Joys of Yiddish*, defines 'borax' under 'shlock' but states the usage only refers to furniture. Partridge states that it is a Canadian term from the 1920s relating to cheap furniture. The *Random House Dictionary* firmly states: 'cheap, showy, poorly-made merchandise, especially cheaply built furniture of an undistinguished or heterogeneous style (so called from the premiums for cheap furniture offered by manufacturers of borax soap)'. However, a family would have had to buy a phenomenal amount of soap to get a worthwhile discount on furniture. There is a large Slavonic input in Yiddish and a prewar colloquial Polish word for to buy on credit was *zborgowac*, which can easily be elided into 'borax'.
J. R. Tarling, London SW15.

QUESTION: Does the company called Dennis make anything other than fire engines?

☐ YES indeed! The brothers John and Raymond Dennis started making bicycles in Guildford in 1895; within a few years they had graduated to motorised bicycles and tricycles, and thence to larger motor vehicles. Production of private cars did not last long, but the company soon became well established in the truck and bus market (and in the manufacture of motor mowers, for which they held a royal warrant for many years). As time went by, truck production was increasingly concentrated on specialised vehicles (such as fire engines, ambulances and refuse collection vehicles) for municipal customers, and a substantial proportion of Dennis bus production was also for municipal fleets. After the Second World War, bus production declined, and Dennis withdrew from this market for a dozen years or so; but they re-entered it in 1978 with considerable success. Since the sale of Leyland Bus to Volvo in 1989, Dennis has been the largest British-owned bus manufacturer, and with the impending closure of the ex-Leyland Bus plant in Workington it will become the largest British-based producer of bus chassis (while still maintaining a strong position in the specialist municipal vehicle market). Production is still based at Guildford, although a move was recently made to a new factory from the Woodbridge Hill works which had been the firm's home since 1905.

(Dr) P. T. Johnstone, St John's College, Cambridge.

☐ FIFTEEN years ago, when I started as a green keeper, the Dennis motor mower was the Rolls-Royce of mowers. It had a massive 36-inch cut and was ideally suited for the preparation of cricket outfields and tennis squares. It was powered by Dennis's own engine, a huge 600 cc side valve which, although beautifully engineered, could be a pig to start on those cold wet April mornings much hated by groundsmen. Looking for nostalgia one autumn, I purchased a 1940s model and spent the winter rebuilding it. Alas, I chose the Easter bank holiday to run it for the first time. It fired up then spluttered and threw out the starting handle, which hit me on the head, resulting in a six-hour wait in casualty for stitches.

Andy Joyce, Southampton.

QUESTION: The 1989 book *The Hangman's Tale: Memoirs of a Public Executioner* refers to the hanging of 22 American servicemen during the war, at Shepton

Mallet in Somerset. How common were such wartime executions? For what crimes had the men been sentenced? How many of them were black?

☐ THE Shepton Mallet hangings were one of many stories about American GIs in Britain. Another was that hospitals in the Bristol area were packed with 'brown babies' – the offspring of white British women and black GIs. Wartime censorship helped to create rumours by default but in this instance the Visiting Forces Act of 1942 was a cause of speculation because it gave the American military authorities exclusive criminal jurisdiction over their armed forces in Britain. Moreover, the American military code specified that rape carried a sentence of death or imprisonment for life, when it was not a capital offence in Britain. This became an issue both inside and outside Parliament in 1944 when there was a feeling that black GIs were being treated by the American authorities more harshly than their white colleagues. Statistics about sentences were notoriously difficult to obtain but some were produced by US Judge Advocate General Edwin McNeil in June 1944. By that date in the European Theatre of Operations eight white Americans and 10 blacks had been convicted of rape. Of these, one black had been executed (though he had also committed a murder) and five were sentenced to life imprisonment. No whites had been executed for rape, though two had been given life sentences. In addition, four whites and 10 blacks were found guilty of murder. Of these, two whites were executed and one given life, whereas five blacks were executed and three given life. In addition, both black and white GIs lost their lives in incidents of inter-racial violence in Britain.

Graham A. Smith (author of When Jim Crow Met John Bull – Black American Soldiers in World War II Britain*), Wolverhampton.*

QUESTION: During the summer of 1961 in Barcelona a juke box favourite, probably by Chuck Berry, had the chorus: 'Hooka-tooka, my soda packer, does your momma chew tobacco?' I have been unsuccessful for three decades in tracking it down. Please tell me it wasn't the figment of a student mind inflamed by vino tinto at four pesetas a litre.

☐ I HAVE a recording of this song, not by Chuck Berry but by Chubby Checker. It is the B-side of 'Loddy Lo' (Cameo-Parkway P890) dated 1963. Have three decades distorted the questioner's memory of the year and name of artist, or is this another version? I don't particularly like the song and normally would give it away. But since the question has generated such interest, and told me that the song is rare enough not to be found after 30 years' search, I shall have to keep it.
Angus McPake, Edinburgh.

QUESTION: Why did the chicken cross the road?

☐ CHICKENS on the road are often not trying to get to the other side. In common with many other birds, they use roads as a source of grit, which is essential in their digestion owing to the rarity of hens' teeth. The grit that birds swallow rests in the part of the digestive system (the crop) where it grinds up their food. Chickens, being omnivorous, may also dine on creatures that failed to make it to the other side.
John Henderson, Chatham, Kent.

☐ I THINK there is a misprint in the question. It should read: 'Why did the chicken cross the rood?' – the answer being, of course, 'to get to the other seed'.
M. E. Owen, Alderholt, Fordingbridge, Hants.

QUESTION: Beethoven's last four quartets have opus numbers 130, 131, 132 and 135. What is opus 134?

☐ BEETHOVEN'S opus 134 is a version for two pianos of his *Grosse Fuge* (op. 133) which had originally been the finale of his B flat quartet (op. 130). The *Grosse Fuge* was not well received at the quartet's first performance – 'music to delight the inhabitants of Morocco', one critic helpfully opined – and Beethoven was furious. His publisher, Matthias Artaria, diplomatically suggested Beethoven prepare a two-piano version of the *Grosse Fuge* and compose a new finale for the quartet. It was not until he had composed the C sharp minor and F major quartets (opp. 131 and 135) that Beethoven provided a substitute finale and the astonishing *Grosse Fuge* was replaced by a shorter allegro movement of glacial cheerfulness. Artaria also published the *Grosse Fuge* (op. 133) and the two-piano version (op. 134), though it remains unclear how well either score sold in Morocco.
Simon Butteriss, London E16.

QUESTION: Who said: 'When I give food to the poor, they call me a saint. When I ask why the poor have no food, they call me a communist'?

☐ IT WAS Dom Helder Camara, Bishop of Recife in the extremely poor north-east of Brazil. In the 1960s this humble monk's siding with the poor rather than the traditional ruling class of the region made him a forerunner of the exponents of Liberation Theology.
Tim Sedgwick-Jell, Whitstable, Kent.

QUESTION: I have just finished reading a novel in which an elderly man is murdered by being suffocated with a pillow. Is this really possible, and wouldn't it be spotted by a pathologist?

☐ IN MY novel, *A Kind of Healthy Grave* (1988), an old man dies as a result of being smothered by a pillow. I was assured by an experienced forensic scientist that this was plausible. *Jessica Mann, Truro, Cornwall.*

☐ THE short answers are 'yes' and 'perhaps', respectively. In fact the example of an elderly person as the victim of such a method of asphyxiation is very appropriate, since it is most often either the old or small children and babies who are killed in such a fashion. Asphyxia causing death is achieved in five distinct ways:

1. Mechanical, such as suffocation with a pillow or the forced flexion of the head on to the chest (in a rugby scrum, for instance); strangulation with hands (quite difficult to do unto death); with a ligature (easier); hanging; or crushing (such as at Ibrox, Heysel or Hillsborough).

2. Toxic, where there is plenty of oxygen but it is prevented from linking with red blood cells. The commonest example is carbon monoxide poisoning, either in exhaust-pipe suicides or in caravans with poor fire ventilation.

3. Environmental, where there is simply not enough air, such as in a locked freezer, a submarine or a confined space where someone has let off a carbon dioxide fire extinguisher.

4. Medically induced, which is done partially by an anaesthetist before an operation. When the balance of oxygen/drug intake is wrong, the result may be asphyxia.

5. Pathological, where a disease restricts oxygen flow from the lungs to the organs. Oedema (fluid) on the lungs, mucus from a dose of bronchitis may do this, especially with older or weaker people. Paraquat poisoning causes death approximately 10 days after contact (licking some will do), as the lungs gradually scar over and breathing becomes progressively impeded.

That it is more vulnerable persons who are most often killed by suffocation with a pillow is no coincidence: the nervous reflexes which cause us to cough, sneeze, roll over or wake up would, in attempted smothering, cause most of us to kick

like a mule. When a person is weaker, through age, infirmity, drink, drugs or disability, the act is more easily accomplished. This 'struggle' or 'force' factor bears too upon the likelihood of detection of such acts. If the nose and mouth are obstructed by hand, say, then it is more likely that a bruise may be left on the points of contact with the victim's face (at times this can show a highly obvious pattern and even the likely size of the killer's hand). With a pillow, a bruise is less likely. This is not necessarily the end of the road, however (except for the victim). People who take longer to die are likely to show small 'pinhead' haemorrhages on the forehead, hairline and eyes. These burst blood vessels are the result of the body going into its final fall-back position: when blood or oxygen supply is restricted, all areas are potentially sacrificed in an attempt to keep the grey matter topped up. In this case, unless death came quickly, the oxygen would be sucked from these blood vessels, causing them to burst, and leaving the smallest but most telling signs. I think the Inspector should be told.
Craig W. Cathcart, Edinburgh.

QUESTION: How do you make a ball bearing spherical?

☐ IT IS already, so you don't.
Simon Walsh, Potters Bar, Herts.

☐ HIGH-carbon steel wire is cut into cylindrical slugs which are stamped between two half-round dies to form a ball with a ridge round its diameter. The ridge is removed by being passed between two cast-iron plates, leaving a rough sphere which is then ground by being rolled round a grooved circular plate against a spinning grinding wheel until the balls are fractionally above the size required. The balls are then hardened and ground again to size. A final lapping process gives them their highly polished finish. The balls are graded by running along two diverging blades and dropping into different pockets, according to size. This is a very accurate process as it is essential that the balls are sized correctly to within thousandths of a millimetre. The balls in an assembled ball bearing must be of exactly the same size to share the load equally, for example on the rotor of a jet engine or machine tool spindle.

N. F. Farrands, Penn, Wolverhampton.

QUESTION: How is it that the vast majority of interrogative words in English – 'what', 'why', 'when', 'where', etc. – begin with the letters 'wh'?

☐ ENGLISH shares with French, Latin, Greek, Russian, Sanskrit and many other mainly European languages a common origin. All these languages are held to be derived from a single unrecorded (and therefore hypothetical) language which we call Indo-European. Among the consonants which could begin a word in Indo-European was the group 'kw', and one group of words which began like that were the closely related group which come into Modern English as interrogatives and relative pronouns. Since these words were related to one another, they almost certainly consisted of a single stem beginning 'kw' to which was added a variety of forms to distinguish the different forms of the interrogative. In some Indo-European languages the 'kw' sequence remained, hence Latin *quis*, etc. However, in the development of the Germanic branch of Indo-European, to which English belongs, the initial 'k' became eventually the breathing sound 'h' (the main part of this process is known as Grimm's Law, after Jakob Grimm of the Brothers Grimm). Thus we find Old English forms such as 'hwa' ('who'). Two later changes have taken place. Firstly, as a result of Norman influence on English spelling, the sequence 'hw' was changed to 'wh' without any corresponding change in pronunciation. Secondly, the 'h' eventually merged with

the 'w' to produce a variant of 'w' which is produced without any vibration of the vocal chords. In many dialects of English this remains, so that there is a contrast between, say, what and watt, but in other dialects, including standard English, there is no contrast. The spelling system, however, very accurately shows the etymological source of each word.
(Prof.) Richard Hogg, Department of English Language and Literature, University of Manchester.

QUESTION: Were there really deck-chairs on the *Titanic*?

☐ YES, they are pictured on page 21 of *Titanic* by Michael McCaughan (Ulster Folk and Transport Museum, 1982).
Richard Bales, Belfast.

QUESTION: Is it true that the braid and buttons on the cuffs of military uniforms were originally intended to prevent servicemen wiping their noses on their sleeves?

☐ I DON'T know, but midshipmen in the Navy were known as 'snotties' and had buttons on their cuffs.
Richard Brown, Retford, Notts.

☐ IF SO, then it doesn't reflect any too well on the personal habits of Admirals of the Fleet and Marshals of the Royal Air Force.
Peter Barnes, Milton Keynes.

QUESTION: How much does the Moon weigh?

☐ WELL, of course the answer is 'nothing at all', since the weight of an object is the net gravitational force acting on a body and, as with all other orbiting objects in the solar system, it is just like an astronaut circling around the Earth: weightless. Weight must be distinguished from mass, which is determined by quantity of material; in the case of the Moon it is about 74 million million million tonnes, according to *Tables of Physical and Chemical Constants*, by Kaye and Laby. At the Earth's surface, a mass of one kilogramme has a weight of one newton due to gravity but if, like the Moon, it is orbiting in space, then it has no weight at all. Incidentally, my physics master at the King's School, Grantham, where Isaac Newton was educated, often reminded us that a force of one newton is about the weight of an apple. A very handy coincidence.

Michael D. Rowe, Offham, Kent.

☐ AS HEAD of physics at Isaac Newton's old school, I am prompted by Mr Rowe's letter to write to explain the misunderstandings he apparently has. Neither an astronaut in orbit round the Earth nor the Moon, which is also in Earth orbit, is weightless, despite the frequent misleading use of the term. As Mr Rowe rightly explains, weight is a force which arises from the gravitational attraction of two bodies and which varies as the inverse square of their distance apart. Zero force, and hence zero weight, will therefore only occur when they are infinitely far apart. The experience of the astronaut is not true weightlessness but he feels weightless because he is in free fall along with his craft. A free-fall parachutist initially experiences the same sensations, as does a high-board diver. In the case of the astronaut and the Moon, the weight force is required to keep them moving in a circle, as required by Newton's first law of motion. It is true that the newton is, conveniently, the approximate weight of an apple but the weight of a mass of 1 kg is actually about 10 N. Both Newton and Mr Rowe were at King's before my time and also before the SI unit system came into general use in schools, which perhaps explains the apparent lapse in his memory, but I would not like anyone to think that we teach

the present generation of budding Newtons incorrect physics.
J. S. Bomphrey, The King's School, Grantham, Lincs.

□ THE head of physics at Isaac Newton's old school he may be, but Mr Bomphrey is surely talking nonsense. Is he not confusing weight and gravity? Gravitational force varies as the inverse square of distance as he rightly says, but what can he mean by saying that the experience of an astronaut 'is not true weightlessness but he feels weightless'? He feels weightless because he is weightless (ignoring the minute attraction to his spacecraft). No experiment he did (short of actually looking out of the window) would enable him to tell that his spacecraft was held, by gravitational force, in orbit around the Earth. Weight is not the force of gravitational attraction, but describes how an object resists gravity. The whole point about orbital free-fall is that the object is not resisting gravity, but is continually accelerating under its influence (the acceleration causing orbital motion, of course, rather than a linear increase in velocity). To use Mr Bomphrey's established analogy, if I pick up an apple I need to apply a force of one newton to hold it up. An astronaut does not need to apply this force, so the apple is weightless. He still needs to apply a force to move it, as it does, of course, continue to have mass. Mr Bomphrey rightly praises the SI system of units which correctly distinguishes between weight and mass. In the Imperial system, with the two different quantities having the same name, there was endless scope for confusion, and for the inventing of alternative obscure units. Whether the Moon is weightless is quite a difficult, and pointless, question to answer. All parts of the Moon are not in free-fall around the Earth, because they are constrained in their orbit by the shape of the Moon. The nearer bits of Moon are moving too slowly for free-fall; the further bits too fast.
David Gibson, Leeds.

☐ THERE is something about physics that makes arguers quite insultingly dismissive of other people's opinions. Mr Bomphrey and Mr Gibson are using different definitions of the word 'weight'; both of them argue correctly from these different definitions. Mr Bomphrey is using the current textbook and physics syllabus definition of 'weight', which says: 'The force of gravity on an object is called its weight' (*GCSE Steps in Physics* by Byron). He is therefore correct to suggest that weightlessness will occur only in situations where the object experiences no gravitational attraction towards other objects. Mr Gibson uses the older definition of weight as described in *Ordinary Level Physics* by Abbott: 'The weight of a body is the force it exerts on anything which freely supports it.' The book goes on to suggest that the body will usually exert this force due to its being attracted towards the centre of the Earth by gravity. This definition makes Mr Gibson's analysis of the situation correct − although suggesting that weight is 'how an object resists gravity' does tend to give the responsibility for weight to the object rather than to that which supports it. The difference in the two views is possibly due to the attempts made over the last 10 years to make physics accessible to a wider proportion of the school population, which has resulted in a simplification of the ideas taught and a significant decrease in the content, which has left Abbott's 'O-level' textbook as a good introduction at A-level to many topics.
Jonathan Parkinson, Head of Physics, St Thomas More School, Blaydon, Northumberland.

QUESTION: What is the first name of Morrissey of the Smiths?

☐ WHEN you are as big as Morrissey, who needs first names?
Emma Douglas, London N12.

☐ THERE are two answers. The first is to say that Morrissey

has two forenames, Steven (with an emphatic 'v') and Patrick. However, the accurate reply is that Morrissey, being a god to hundreds of thousands of daffodil-wielding poetic teenagers (many now in their early to mid-twenties), has no first name and is to be revered as the purely hermaphrodite and transparent-shirt-wearing 'Morrissey'.

Mark Brown, Glasgow.

□ BACK in the mid-eighties, when the Smiths first exploded on to the scene (those were the days), I seem to remember the alternative spelling of Stephen being used in the press, as well as names like Dave, Mike and John by the more ignorant members of the media (i.e. Radio 1 DJs). I also recall a bizarre occurrence when, at the height of Smiths mania, someone found a Steven Patrick Morrissey living in a suburb of Manchester (from which city the Smiths hailed) and the unfortunate chap, a self-employed builder or something, was besieged by lovelorn young men and women, thinking that he was their hero. Or was this an apocryphal story?

Stephen F. Dent, Bath.

QUESTION: Is it possible to cross-breed between a Bactrian camel and a dromedary? If so, would the offspring have one hump or two?

□ YES it is, and one hump. Hybrid camels have been bred for centuries, mainly by Turkish peoples, in the broad belt of south-western Asia where the habitats of the two species meet, including Anatolia, Syria, northern Iran and Afghanistan. In the present century hybridisation was systematically pursued in the former Soviet Union. The hybrid is a magnificent beast, with the best qualities of each, larger and stronger than either of the parents, an ideal pack animal capable of carrying nearly half a ton, though it is virtually sterile. In some parts of Turkey and northern Afghanistan

male hybrids are specially bred for camel-fights. An excellent and readable account of the history, distribution and practices of camel hybridisation can be found in Richard Bulliet's *The Camel and the Wheel* (Harvard University Press, 1975); a new edition has recently appeared, I believe. *(Dr) R. L. Tapper, School of Oriental and African Studies, London WC1.*

QUESTION: In Hitchcock's version of *The Thirty-Nine Steps*, there is a music-hall scene in which 'Mr Memory' answers questions from the audience. One man persistently asks 'What causes pip in poultry?' but his question is ignored. Can anyone else tell me the answer?

☐ HAD he known the answer, Mr Memory would have told his persistent inquirer that pip in poultry was caused by the fowl breathing through its mouth (beak) as a result of a respiratory disease, such as catarrh, roup or diphtheria. In over 40 years as a poultry keeper I have never had a case or heard of anyone else coming across it. Indeed, although having a fairly extensive library of books on poultry, ancient and modern, in only two could I find a description of pip. The best was in the oldest of my collection, W. B. Teget-meier's *Poultry Book*, second edition, 1872. The author trained as a doctor but gave up practice to become a naturalist. He assisted Darwin in his researches into the vari-ations of animals, and became nature editor of the *Field*. According to him, pip caused the tongue to become hard and horny and in some parts of the country the remedy was to snip off the end of the tongue, a practice he described as use-less and barbarous. An American book published in 1933 is the only other one I have that describes pip and concurs with Tegetmeier that it is a symptom of respiratory diseases. *P. R. Ricketts, Swindon, Wilts.*

QUESTION: Can a person like Wagner's music and still be a socialist?

□ *THE Perfect Wagnerite*, George Bernard Shaw's book, argues that Wagner's *Ring* cycle is a political allegory offer-ing a critique of capitalism. For Shaw, the Gods are to be interpreted as the aristocracy, the Giants as peasants, the Nibelungs as the proletariat and Alberich as a capitalist. Even Siegfried, the sword-wielding superman himself, is a model for a free socialist 'New Man', destined to destroy this oppressive system. Unfortunately, Shaw says, Wagner comes over all soppy at the crucial moment and the allegory collapses into a lot of gush about redemption through love. Nevertheless the *Ring* gives us some idea of what a future socialist art might be like. This may seem odd given Wagner's later association with Nazism but it must be remembered that at this time socialist and fascist ideas actually overlapped in many areas. Wagner had some pretty

unpleasant opinions, mainly in his later years, but he also believed in the prospect of an art which would recapture the relationship between popular appeal and cultural sophistication which had existed in Shakespeare's day. He wanted the widest possible audience to be in touch with the musical inheritance of Beethoven and with the power of drama which combined the achievements of Sophocles and Shakespeare. In these days of post-modern cultural fragmentation and consumer culture, that's not a bad vision of a truly socialist art.
Julie Byrne, Liverpool 18.

□ TRY listening to the works of the right-on composer of revolutionary people's 'music', Cornelius Cardew. You'll be desperate for the politically dubious pleasure of *Parsifal* in no time.
John Sheldon, Liverpool 1.

□ IF WAGNER is suspect, where does that leave Chopin (a virulent anti-Semite), Puccini (an honorary member of the Italian Fascist Party) and Stravinsky (who revered Mussolini)? As D. H. Lawrence said: 'Don't judge the artist, trust the tale.'
Jonathan Yglesias, London N10.

□ BRAHMS is known to have entertained very right-wing views, yet this did not prevent the Labour Party adopting a pop version of his First Symphony during its television broadcasts for the 1987 election. Conversely, the music of that good socialist Gustav Holst formed the background to the Tories' party political broadcasts in the same year.
Walter Cairns, Manchester 20.

QUESTION: In the mid-1930s the BBC banned a pair of comedians called Clapham and Dwyer after they allegedly broadcast an improper joke. A schoolboy at the

time, I did not understand the joke and for the life of me cannot remember it now. Can anyone help?

☐ I WAS also a schoolboy at the time but perhaps a more mature one. Clapham (the 'straight man') was purporting to give a lecture on desert irrigation and Dwyer was pretending to be hard of hearing. Clapham said: 'You look at the baking waste and wonder what will be there in a few months' time.' Dwyer repeated this as: 'You look at a lady's waist and wonder what will be there in a few months' time.' This was taken to refer to pregnancy, which decent people (as represented by the BBC under Sir John Reith) did not talk about. The pair contended, however, that it was a joke about Paris fashions. This attitude continued at the BBC even during the war, when C. E. M. Joad got into trouble for quoting a saying of Confucius: 'What is the use of going to bed early to save candles if the result be twins?'
Eric Masel, London N2.

☐ CLAPHAM and Dwyer were banned for five months in 1935 after a complaint from a vicar about one of their jokes in *Music Hall*, the most popular entertainment show on radio at the time. And the joke? 'What is the difference between a champagne cork and a baby?' Answer: 'A champagne cork has the maker's name on its bottom.' This produced the following announcement in the BBC's early evening news bulletin (21 January 1935): 'The BBC apologises to listeners for the inclusion in the *Music Hall* programme . . . of certain highly objectionable remarks, violating standards which have been firmly established by the practice of the BBC.' By this time the BBC had forbidden jokes containing references to politics and politicians, advertisements, drink and prohibition in the US, clergymen, medical matters and human infirmities, Scotsmen and Welshmen but not, apparently, Irishmen. Also excluded were jokes about sea-sickness, flat feet, cheese, kippers and bunions. For further details see

Scannell and Cardiff, *A Social History of British Broadcast-ing* (Blackwell, 1991, pp. 226–7).
Paddy Scannell, Oxford.

QUESTION: *Black's Medical Dictionary* **says that a person with extremely foul breath is generally unaware of it. Is there any way to test one's own breath, or must one wait until someone else has the courage to say something?**

☐ ACCORDING to Philip Hodson, agony uncle on the 'Grow-ing Pains' slot of *Going Live* (BBC Saturday morning kids' programme), you should lick the palm of your hand and then sniff it. I have tried this – and it works. What does not work is to exhale into your cupped hands and then sniff – the pongy air molecules disperse into the wider atmosphere too fast.
Adrienne Wyper, London SE5.

☐ AS THE commonest cause is unhealthy gums, self-diagno-sis can be performed by running the fingernail of a clean hand under the edge of the gum and then smelling the nail. Where traces of a foul odour are detected, massage of the affected gum will alleviate the problem. However, this is useless when the odour is caused by garlic: one must accept that one's breath niffs to heaven and retire from society for 24 hours.
H. Price, Porthmadog, Gwynedd.

QUESTION: Who invented the sash window and what are its virtues? Why did builders not adopt the inward-opening French window, which is simpler and more easily cleaned?

☐ MOST probably, sash windows were not 'invented' but

developed from the simpler horizontal sliding sash (known today as the 'Yorkshire' sash). They are supposed to have come from Holland in the seventeenth century. However, W. Horman, in his *Vulgaria*, printed in 1519, writes: 'Glasen wyndowis let in the lyght . . . I have many prety wyndowes shette with levys goynge up and down.' They were first used conspicuously at Chatsworth in 1676–80 and then in 1685 at the Banqueting House at Whitehall, designed by Inigo Jones, where they replaced the original casement (i.e. side-hung) windows. They became exceedingly popular; earlier windows were replaced with sashes, and sashes were used almost exclusively in new buildings, from cottages to palaces, throughout Britain and the colonies, until early this century. This phenomenal 250-year success story is due to the many excellent qualities of the sash window. For instance, the opening of the window can be finely adjusted, down to a narrow gap at the top or the bottom or both, giving good control of ventilation with little danger of rain blowing into the room. A 'French' window or inward open-ing casement is very vulnerable in this respect, and would be quite unsuited to British weather. The sash, being hung from each of its top corners, rather than from the side as with a hinged window, is less likely to distort under its own weight. This has several consequences. Less distortion means longer life: there are many sash windows still serviceable after 150 years or more. Imagine a 150-year-old plastic window! Casement windows need wider components for stiffness. Larger casement windows need two lights (the moving parts) which necessarily meet side by side in the centre and so, from the visual point of view, give a strong central vertical emphasis. The wooden structure of the sash, on the other hand, can be made with thinner sections, giving more light and a more delicate appearance, and could be vertic-ally divided into three panes, harmonising with the clas-sical style and so becoming the principal feature of the graceful and elegant buildings of the Queen Anne and Georgian periods. Sash windows are less highly regarded today than they were, but they are very much victims of their longevity; that rattling, draughty but unopenable old window may well have functioned beautifully for the first 100 years of its life; but in refusing to die gracefully has become the victim of inexperienced tradesmen and heavy-handed DIYers. A new plastic window will need replacing entirely in about 20 years; in the same period a new sash window will probably only need new cords, if that.

Jacob Butler, Joiner, Bonsall, Derbyshire.

QUESTION: Is it dangerous to swallow chewing-gum?

☐ SWALLOWED chewing-gum is excreted in the usual way, and to my knowledge constitutes no hazard. However, aspiration of gum into the respiratory tract, as may happen during violent exertion, particularly if associated with a blow to the chest causing a sudden involuntary intake of breath, is a serious matter. Such accidents typically occur during contact sports like rugby. If the gum lodges in the bronchi, wheezing and infection result; if it sticks in the trachea, fatal asphyxia can ensue. Chewing during these activities is thus highly inadvisable. Such episodes are almost unknown in cricket, despite the near-universal chomping. However, it was reported in the *Lancet* that during the Adelaide Test in 1979, Australian batsman Darling, struck on the chest by a ball from England's Willis, 'collapsed, choked on his chewing gum'. Only prompt medical attention prevented serious consequences.

(Dr) Robert Heys, Ripponden, Halifax.

QUESTION: Why do BR diesel locomotives spend long periods ticking over in stations, rather than switching off and keeping stations fume-free?

☐ IT HAS nothing to do with fumes but is to ensure the

complete inaudibility of the loudspeaker announcements. *Michael J. Smith, Swaffham, Norfolk.*

☐ DIESEL locomotives keep their engines ticking over to stop their batteries from going flat. A diesel engine does not have spark plugs, as its power comes from ignition of a fuel/air mixture by the pressure of a piston, operated by a crankshaft, which operates the engine, which operates the crankshaft. So to get power out of the diesel engine, you have to feed some in, which is done with electric starter motors that turn the crankshaft. In diesel road vehicles, car-type batteries are used, but the large locomotive engines need large batteries that cost many thousands of pounds. Should these be damaged or run down, you're left with a hundred tons of dead locomotive blocking a railway line. To prevent that calamity, the engines, once started, are kept running as long as possible. This is safer and cheaper than frequently starting and stopping the engines with resultant wear and tear on the batteries. Any smoke produced is a sign of poor engine maintenance, as the good Dr Diesel designed his engine to be eco-friendly.
Ray Vickers, Huddersfield.

☐ RAY Vickers is wrong. Keeping locomotives on tickover does not stop the batteries from going flat. It might make sure that the batteries are at their full rated capacity, but this is not the same thing. His confused explanation of the workings of internal combustion engines (whether they be spark-ignition or compression-ignition) does nothing to clarify his main point, which is that you start any type of mobile internal combustion engine by means of a battery. Spark-ignition engines can, for several reasons, use a smaller and cheaper battery than is used by compression-ignition engines. Making sure that the larger batteries are kept topped up to their capacity therefore makes economic sense (though I cannot see why it should be safer). One point

which he misses is that this practice is nowadays more or less seasonal. Locos are usually turned off in hot weather to avoid problems should the cooling systems fail, but kept running in cold weather so that the engine, rather than the batteries, can be used to power ancillary functions such as fuel-tank heaters. In cold weather, these heaters stop fuel oil from coagulating (the Achilles heel of road transport equivalents). Tickover on the engines also avoids engine freezing problems in cold weather. Battery failure need not necessarily incapacitate a diesel locomotive. Though jump-starting might be impossible in practice, diesel locomotives can be bump-started by towing, just like cars. Smoke from a compression-ignition exhaust usually denotes clogged or untuned injectors – often a sign of poor maintenance of existing plant or lack of investment in new machinery. I do not recall ever reading that Dr Rudolf Diesel was concerned about the environment (except to the extent of becoming part of it in mysterious circumstances during a cross-Channel trip in 1912). Since his first engines used had an inefficient working cycle, with powdered coal as their fuel, I cannot see that he achieved any such end, no matter what his intentions. And what are referred to as Diesel should be called 'Ackroyd-Stuart' engines. The English engineer of the first decade of this century was responsible for the development of compression-ignition engines into a far more practicable and successful power plant than the Diesel equivalent.
J. B. Woods, York.

QUESTION: Why is swooning out of fashion?

☐ SWOONING was never in fashion; tight corsetting was, however. The resulting restriction caused fainting, particularly in moments of stress or excitement when the woman would attempt to breathe deeply and be prevented from taking in the required amount of air by the corsets. This practice is seen by many as one of oppression, similar to that

of foot-binding, for example, and as a means of controlling women.
Elizabeth d'Lasselle, Barnet, Herts.

QUESTION: Why did Shakespeare make Julius Caesar's last words the Latin 'Et tu, Brute?' when Suetonius tells us they were the Greek 'Kai su, teknon?' (You too, my son?)? Plutarch, on the other hand, says that Caesar died in silence, pulling his toga over his head.

□ THE answer is simple. The ancient historians such as Suetonius and Plutarch were as much in the entertainment business as the great playwright. Phrases like Suetonius' 'Kai su, teknon' and Plutarch's dramatic descriptions were as much for the enjoyment of the reader/listener as for the true recording of fact. Shakespeare simply used the line 'Et tu, Brute?' because it suited his dramatic purpose, just as Plutarch and Suetonius had used what suited them. Personally, I suspect Julius Caesar's last words were 'aaaaaaaaaaah'.
Jonathan Munn, Whitchurch, Cardiff.

□ I THINK it's generally accepted that Caesar's dying words were the Greek 'Kai su, teknon'. Romans of his class moved easily between Latin and Greek. But it's important to recognise that he was not asking 'You too, my son?' The words 'Kai su' – found in Greek comedy and on mosaics – mean 'Screw you!' and the 'teknon' ('kid') just makes it fiercer.
Greg Rowe, The Queen's College, Oxford.

□ I MUST point out that Shakespeare does not make Caesar's last words 'Et tu, Brute?' Shakespeare gives him another three words after the famous quotation: 'Then fall, Caesar!'
Eric Standidge, London SE10.

INDEX